SELF-DEFENSE
NERVE CENTERS & PRESSURE POINTS is based on modern concepts of self-defense; the point of view is ethical, humanistic and rational.

The results of self-defense actions are described in the most accurate way possible, taking into account the factors of relative size, strength, health and emotional control.

Current knowledge of physiology and anatomy is applied to this subject which has long been much obscured by superstition, myth and legend. The facts and the fantasies of the "deadly" blows are examined and evaluated.

Appropriate body targets for practical self-defense are compared with point targets used in stylized martial arts and in sport tournament.

For the teacher and student of self-defense or of any style of any specialty of the martial arts this book is an important reference source.

". . . a practical guide to the most effective weaponless self-defense using the least possible force. . ."

THE POLICE CHIEF

BOOKS by BRUCE TEGNER

BRUCE TEGNER'S COMPLETE BOOK of SELF-DEFENSE

SELF-DEFENSE: A BASIC COURSE

SELF-DEFENSE NERVE CENTERS & PRESSURE POINTS

DEFENSE TACTICS for LAW ENFORCEMENT
Weaponless Defense & Control and Baton Techniques

STICK-FIGHTING: SELF-DEFENSE

STICK-FIGHTING: SPORT FORMS

KUNG FU & TAI CHI

SAVATE: FRENCH FOOT & FIST FIGHTING

KARATE & JUDO EXERCISES

BRUCE TEGNER'S COMPLETE BOOK of JUJITSU

JUDO: BEGINNER to BLACK BELT

KARATE: BEGINNER to BLACK BELT

AIKIDO & BOKATA

BOOKS by BRUCE TEGNER & ALICE McGRATH

SELF-DEFENSE & ASSAULT PREVENTION for GIRLS & WOMEN

SELF-DEFENSE for YOUR CHILD
Elementary school age boys & girls

SOLO FORMS of KARATE, TAI CHI, AIKIDO & KUNG FU

BOOKS by Ellen Kei Hua

KUNG FU MEDITATIONS & Chinese Proverbial Wisdom

MEDITATIONS of the MASTERS

COMPLETELY NEW VERSION

SELF-DEFENSE NERVE CENTERS & PRESSURE POINTS

FOR KARATE, JUJITSU & ATEMI-WAZA

By BRUCE TEGNER

THOR PUBLISHING COMPANY
VENTURA CA 93002

Library of Congress Cataloging in Publication Data

Tegner, Bruce.
Self-defense nerve centers & pressure points: for karate, jujitsu & atemi-waza.

Includes index
1. Self-defense. I. Title.
GV1111.T423 1978 796.8'15 78-18169
ISBN 0-87407-519-X
ISBN 0-87407-029-5 pbk.

SELF-DEFENSE NERVE CENTERS & PRESSURE POINTS
First edition: September 1968
Revised edition: September 1978
Seventeenth printing: January 1994

THOR PUBLISHING COMPANY
P.O. BOX 1782
VENTURA, CA 93002

PRINTED IN U.S.A.

ACKNOWLEDGMENTS

The material for this book was collected over many years with the help of many people. My students, and friends in civilian and military police work provided personal observations and reports, for which I am grateful.

The late V. E. Christensen, M.D. helped me in the preparation of an earlier version of this book by assisting me in researching accident and injury reports and by allowing me to observe and question him during post-mortem examinations. Dr. Christensen had an active interest in sports medicine. He had studied kung fu and aikido and he held a black belt rank in karate. He was a valuable consultant and a valued friend. He is remembered with appreciation and affection.

For the present version I have had the assistance of H. O'Neil Zeigler, an instructor of comparative anatomy and physiology, who gave suggestions for updating the material, and of Dick Schumacher, whose specialty is evaluation of sport-related injury. I am grateful to them for useful discussions and comments and for their generosity and kindness.

Most of the photos illustrating the striking areas are of RICHARD WINDISHAR.

The photos showing some examples of defense actions are taken from:
BRUCE TEGNER'S COMPLETE BOOK of SELF-DEFENSE
SELF-DEFENSE for YOUR CHILD
SELF-DEFENSE & ASSAULT PREVENTION for GIRLS & WOMEN
all of which are published by Thor Publishing Company, Ventura, California.

Drawings on pages 114,116,117 and 119 are by KEVIN MILLER

BRUCE TEGNER BOOKS REVIEWED

KARATE: BEGINNER to BLACK BELT

"Techniques and routines...illustrated in profuse detail...a fine introduction and a worthwhile reference source...specially geared to a YA audience." KLIATT YOUNG ADULT PB BOOK GUIDE

SELF-DEFENSE: A BASIC COURSE

"An eminently practical, concise guide to self-defense...for young men..." American Library Association BOOKLIST

"YA - A calm, nonsexist approach to simple yet effective self-defense techniques...clear photographs...sound advice."
SCHOOL LIBRARY JOURNAL

BRUCE TEGNER'S COMPLETE BOOK OF JUJITSU

"...authoritative and easy-to-follow text..."
SCHOOL LIBRARY JOURNAL

BRUCE TEGNER'S COMPLETE BOOK OF SELF-DEFENSE

Recommended for Y.A. in the American Library Association
BOOKLIST

SELF-DEFENSE & ASSAULT PREVENTION FOR GIRLS & WOMEN (with Alice McGrath)

"...should be required reading for all girls and women..."
WILSON LIBRARY BULLETIN

"...simple and straightforward with no condescension...easy to learn and viable as defense tactics..." SCHOOL LIBRARY JOURNAL

SELF-DEFENSE FOR YOUR CHILD (with Alice McGrath)

[For elementary school-age boys & girls]

"...informative, readable book for family use..."
CHRISTIAN HOME & SCHOOL

DEFENSE TACTICS FOR LAW ENFORCEMENT

"...a practical tool for police academy programs, police programs at the university level, and for the (individual) officer..."
THE POLICE CHIEF

KUNG FU & TAI CHI: Chinese Karate and Classical Exercise

"...recommended for physical fitness collections."
LIBRARY JOURNAL

SOLO FORMS of Karate, Tai Chi, Aikido & Kung Fu (with Alice McGrath)

"...well-coordinated, step-by-step instructions...carefully captioned photos...for personal enjoyment and exercise..." YA
American Library Association BOOKLIST

STICK-FIGHTING: SPORT FORMS

"...illustrations and directions are clear and easy to follow... based on foil fencing, quarterstaff and broadsword...in addition to sports-oriented use...might prove of value to drama students..."
American Library Association BOOKLIST

CONTENTS

INTRODUCTION by ALICE McGRATH

WHAT IS SELF-DEFENSE? 11
WHAT ARE NERVE CENTERS & PRESSURE POINTS? 12
SUPERSTITION OR KNOWLEDGE 13
KARATE, JUJITSU & ATEMI-WAZA 14
COMPARISON OF FIGHTING SYSTEMS CHART 15
PAIN & THE PSYCHODYNAMICS OF SELF-DEFENSE 16
THE MYTHS OF THE DEADLY BLOWS 18
CAN NASAL BONES BE DRIVEN INTO THE BRAIN? 18
PLUCKING OUT THE HEART OR SPINE 19
TOUCH-OF-DEATH 19
THE MEDIA 20
HAND CONDITIONING IS NOT NECESSARY! 21
ACCURACY OF THE DESCRIPTIONS 22
COMPARING THE EFFECTS OF BLOWS 24
WEAPONS 26
MOVIE & TV FIGHT SCENES 32

NERVE CENTERS & PRESSURE POINTS

TEMPLE AREA 34
ONTO THE NOSE 36
SIDE OF THE NOSE 38
UP UNDER THE NOSE 39
EYES 40
UP UNDER THE CHIN 41
AT THE EAR 42
UP UNDER THE EAR 42
WINDPIPE/ADAM'S APPLE 43
UP UNDER THE JAW 44
THROAT HOLLOW 44
SIDE OF THE NECK 46
MUSCLE AT THE BASE OF THE NECK 48
COLLARBONE 48
BASE OF THE SKULL 50
BASE OF THE NECK 50
BETWEEN THE SHOULDER BLADES 52
KIDNEY AREA 53
SOLAR PLEXUS 54
SIDE OF THE BODY, UNDER LAST RIB 56

INSIDE OF ELBOW JOINT 58
OUTSIDE OF ELBOW JOINT 58
FOREARM MOUND 60
WRIST 62
BACK OF UPPER ARM 62
LOWER FOREARM 64
BACK OF THE HAND 65
LOWER ABDOMINAL AREA 66
GROIN 66
UPPER INNER THIGH 68
KNEE 69
BACK OF THE KNEE 72
SHIN 74
INSTEP 76
ANKLE 77
COCCYX 78
BACK OF THE THIGH 78
CALF 80
ACHILLES' TENDON 81

SUPPLEMENT

LOCATING THE TARGET 82
"BEST" TARGET AREAS 86
ACCURACY & SPEED PRACTICE PROCEDURES 88
HITTING A SMALL MOVING OBJECT 88
FULL-CONTACT STRIKING BAG 91
HITTING STICK 92
HOOP STICK 93
MEMORIZE TARGET AREAS 94
FIGHTING STANCES: WHY & WHEN 98
WRESTLING STANCE 99
JUDO CONTEST STANCE 100
KARATE STANCES 101
POINT TARGETS IN COMBAT SPORTS 104
STYLES OF KARATE 105
KARATE CONTEST POINTS 106
KARATE MODERNIZED 107
TENDONS, LIGAMENTS & JOINTS 120
INDEX 124

ANATOMICAL DRAWINGS 35, 115, 116, 117, 119

INTRODUCTION

WHAT IS SELF-DEFENSE?

A modern definition of self-defense is in order. One way of defining self-defense is to explain what it is *not*. Personal self-defense is not warfare; it is not vengeance; it is not an art; it is not a sporting event; it is not a movie or television fight scene.

Self-defense is preparation to minimize the possibility of assault. It is training to learn and use appropriate and effective physical actions if there is no practical available alternative.

Self-defense instruction is the beginning of a process of learning how to avoid becoming a victim.

Many victims of assault are victims not because they lack the capacity to win fights but because they have been given absolutely no preparation to cope with this special kind of emergency.

The old-fashioned view that self-defense instruction is training to reach a high level of fighting skill has the effect of eliminating those individuals who have the greatest need. It is precisely those people who are unable or unwilling to become fierce fighting machines who benefit from practical self-defense instruction to the greatest degree.

Our capabilities ought to bear some relationship to real-life objectives. People learning to defend themselves against assault ought not to be trained as though they were preparing for warfare. The concepts, techniques and methods appropriate for training Samurai warriors are not those appropriate for teaching self-defense as a practical skill for today.

The legal and moral definition of self-defense expressly limits the degree of force to the *least* which can be used to avert, stop, or escape from an intended assault.

In old-style self-defense, every assault is viewed as a very vicious assault. Real life is different. There are degrees of danger. Assault intentions range from mildly threatening to the intent to do great bodily harm. More important, there are mildly threatening situations which, if handled properly with assertive self-control, can be prevented from escalating into physical violence.

There must be a full range of responses to correspond to the range of possible situations. Otherwise there is only the all-or-nothing response, which is not a choice -- it is a dilemma. The person who cannot cope with a mildly threatening hostile act does nothing, or responds to the mild threat as if it were a vicious assault. If the intended victim is passive it encourages the assailant and assaultive action is more likely to occur. Reacting to a mild threat as though it were a vicious assault is inappropriate.

The objective of ethical self-defense instruction is to teach appropriate and effective responses. The objective of this book is to give information and guidance toward making those appropriate responses.

WHAT ARE NERVE CENTERS & PRESSURE POINTS?

"Nerve centers" and "pressure points" are not scientific descriptions of anatomical entities. They are layman's terms which we use for everyday discussion of this aspect of our subject.

Nerve center is used to describe body areas which are most susceptible to pain sensation on most people because of a concentration of relatively exposed nerves. In this sense the shin is a nerve center. Not all nerves are carriers of impulses experienced as pain, so not all concentrations of nerves produce a nerve center in our terms. The buttocks have a high concentration of nerves, but this area is ordinarily one of the least sensitive.

Pressure point, in this text, indicates an area which is peculiarly vulnerable to injury or incapacitating pain. An example is the windpipe.

SUPERSTITION OR KNOWLEDGE

The Asian fighting skills were practiced and developed many centuries prior to the discovery of the actual nature of vital body functions such as the process of digestion and the circulation of the blood.

Among the ancients, muscle contractions, palpitations, intestinal growling and other such internal stirrings and audible processes were thought to result from reptile spirits which resided within the body and that these hyperphysical serpents and dragons moved about in response to specific human activity.

We ought to be careful about accepting ancient ideas as truth merely because they are old. We may not have made much progress toward an understanding of the human psyche, but we do know a great deal more now than we used to know about our physical structure and our body functions.

If you are seriously interested in this subject field you should make a reasonably thorough study of anatomy and of the mechanics of the human body.

If you expect to be involved in self-defense instruction, even on an informal, nonprofessional club or group basis, you have an absolute responsibility to be informed. There are too many people in this field who are uninformed and who are circulating ancient superstitions and misconceptions. The only way to refute ignorance is with knowledge.

Take courses in anatomy and physiology, if you can. In many areas there are free adult education programs at the high school level. If you cannot take a formal class, use your local library for a self-directed study program using the reference books you will find there.

KARATE, JUJITSU & ATEMI-WAZA

Martial arts is an omnibus term used to designate many different styles of weaponless fighting as well as systems of armed fighting. As the term is now used, it refers only to those fighting styles which developed in Asian countries. It would be more accurate to include among the martial arts the skills which were originally used for combat regardless of the country or region in which they were developed. Fencing, wrestling, boxing and archery are martial arts in exactly the same sense that judo, kendo, karate, aikido and kung fu are martial arts.

There are literally hundreds of styles and substyles of the weaponless martial arts but there is a relatively small group of techniques utilized in all of them. The major groups of techniques are: Grappling and bending and twisting the joints (judo, aikido, wrestling); throwing and tripping and takedowns (judo, wrestling); hand blows (boxing); hand and foot blows (karate, jujitsu, kung fu, savate, atemi-waza, Tai boxing).

Although there are many styles and substyles of karate and kung fu, all of the styles utilize the techniques of hitting and kicking at nerve centers and pressure points. Although there are hundreds of styles of jujitsu, most of them include techniques of hitting and kicking at nerve centers and pressure points. Atemi-waza is solely concerned with techniques of hitting and kicking at specific nerve center and pressure point body targets.

The general term *martial arts* and the specialty terms such as *karate*, *kung fu*, *judo*, *jujitsu*, *aikido* and other names for the Asian-style fighting skills are used indiscriminately by the lay public. For an overview of the subject field and clarification of some of the differences and similarities among the specialties see the current edition of the *Encyclopedia Americana* which is available for reference at most public libraries.

COMPARISON of FIGHTING SYSTEMS

	ATEMI-WAZA	BOXING	JUDO	JUJITSU	KARATE & KUNG FU	SAVATE	WRESTLING
Fist blows, blocks & parries	★	★		★	★	★	
Open hand & arm blows	★			★	★	★	
High kicks				★	★	★	
Low kicks	★			★		★	
Holds, locks & grappling			★	★			★
Throws			★	★			
Takedowns			★	★	★		★
Nerve centers & pressure points emphasized	★			★	★		
Training emphasizes flexible response rather than rigid, prearranged actions		★	★			★	★

For convenience we speak of pain as something which is inflicted. In fact, pain is a more complicated matter. Pain involves two factors--one is the application of a stimulus and the other is the response to the stimulus.

There is an astonishing range of responses to exactly the same stimulus. There are people who go to the dentist calmly and are able to think about something else while dental work is being done. Others go to the dentist in a state of fearful agitation and endure dental work in acute agony. There are individuals who can present themselves for injections or innoculations with no sign of anxiety. There are others who faint each time they get a shot.

There are individuals whose fear and anxiety about physical violence is so intense that the idea of the possibility of assault is terrifying. For these people the stimulus of a blow would probably provoke a very high response of pain. Fearful, anxious individuals will experience an assault with greater trauma than those who have a higher tolerance for pain.

Just as different individuals respond differently to the blows of an assault, different individuals will respond in different ways to the blows of a physical defense action.

The basic concept in old-style self-defense training is that one must develop an extremely high level of fighting skill. That concept derives from combat-oriented training. For combat it is necessary to have the ability to win fights and to have the capacity for inflicting maximum pain.

But pain is only one of the factors in self-defense. As important as the ability to inflict pain is an understanding of the psychological interaction between the assailant and the intended victim.

The relationships in self-defense are very different from those in combat or in combat sports. It is a mistake to view the three entirely different events as though they were the same. In most sport contests it is not necessary to inflict any pain in order to win. In battle it is necessary to wound, incapacitate or kill the opponent in order to win. The amount of pain necessary in practical self-defense is only that which convinces the would-be assailant that a spirited and orderly defense will be made and that the intended victim will not be passive.

Effective self-defense, in many instances, does not even involve inflicting pain or resorting to physical actions. When physical actions are appropriate, they might result in little pain, very great pain, or not pain at all!

Self-control, determined resistance, a refusal to accept the role of victim are factors which could be much more important for your safety and well-being than the ability to inflict pain.

The person who chooses a helpless or seemingly vulnerable individual as an object for physical violence is not brave. In many instances of threatened assault the first indication of refusal to be a passive victim is enough to deter the assailant. This refusal might be verbal (no pain at all) or it might, in the event of a serious assault, involve responding with a forceful blow.

The ability to refrain from using physical actions and the ability to inflict appropriate pain are equally important. It is not necessary to be a highly trained fighter in order to present yourself as competent and self-reliant. Gesture, attitude, language and tone can convey the message that you refuse the role of passive victim. An assertive and convincing manner of responding to the threat of assault will reduce significantly the carrying out of the threat.

THE MYTHS OF THE DEADLY BLOWS

Legend, fantasy, tall tales, movie and television fight scenes and ignorance have all contributed to the misconceptions and cult stories about the secret deadly blows known only to an elect few of the masters of the martial arts.

Among the myths, legends and misconceptions which are solemnly repeated as though they were factual are those of the master who could reach in with his dagger hand and pluck out a still-beating heart, or pull the spine out of the living body of his adversary. There is the tale of the death without contact and the terrible and mysterious seven-year death. One of the most widely circulated misconceptions is that a blow upward under the nose can cause death by driving the nasal bones into the brain.

CAN NASAL BONES BE DRIVEN INTO THE BRAIN?

This piece of nonsense can be disproved by looking at the human skull structure in an anatomy book, or by examining a skull in an anatomy class.

Any sufficiently powerful blow to the head could be fatal. But the cause of death from a forceful blow up under the nose would not be related to nasal bones driven into the brain. Fatality would result from shock transmitted to the brain.

Most of the nose is not bone but cartilage. The bones of the nose are more fragile than the surrounding skull structure. A forceful blow would fracture the nasal bones more easily than it would fracture the skull. Even if the nasal bones were intact there is no channel through which they could enter the brain. The only entrances to the brain from the angle of an upward blow are the passages for nerves and blood vessels and they are much too small to accommodate nasal bones.

So while it is possible to deliver a fatal blow by striking up under the nose, death would not result from bones entering the brain but from concussion or ruptured blood vessels.

PLUCKING OUT THE HEART OR SPINE

Every culture has its suprahuman heroes, demi-gods and legendary figures. Myth is part of all cultures and it serves a serious purpose -- part poetic, part prophetic. Myths create an orderly past and give us a sense of a future in which we are greater than we can ever be today.

There is a danger in regarding legend as literal truth. If you believe everything -- without verification -- it will dull your ability to distinguish fantasy from fact, lies from truth. A credulous person - one who does not ask questions and demand verifiable proof -- is in a perilous position. As a consumer, as a voter, as a participant in a highly complex society, it is your duty and in your survival interest to be able to tell the difference between fantasy and reality, between promotional hucksterism and plain fact.

So, if you approach the tales of the karate masters as wonderful Asian folklore - fine! The problem is that too many people believe that they are factual.

The chilling tale of the karate master with the power to reach into a human body and pluck out the heart or spine can only be taken as legend. It is patently absurd to think of proving or disproving it. Better to leave it where it belongs, along with the exploits of Paul Bunyan and John Henry.

TOUCH-OF-DEATH

The touch-of-death story is clearly a tale of magic. The possessor of this mysterious power to cause death by merely touching at a secret spot has never been seen nor has any victim ever been identified. This is a great story for entertainment-by-fright.

A variation of the touch-of-death legend is the seven-year death. In this version the master possesses the power to touch or to strike at an adversary so that death occurs seven years later.

It is conceivable that in a fight there could be internal injury leading to deterioration or malfunction of a vital organ and that death could follow after an interval. That would be an accident. But the seven-year death tale does not assign the possibility of accident. What it proposes is that someone with secret powers could predetermine the exact degree of injury, deliver exactly the right amount of force at precisely the spot to cause a lingering death at a specified future time. There is no acceptable proof of such a possibility.

There is no secret to it. Anyone who can deliver a forceful blow of any style to a vulnerable part of the body is capable of delivering a "deadly" blow. A boxing blow of sufficient force is as deadly as a karate or kung fu blow of equal force.

THE MEDIA

Entertainment movies and television shows do not make claims to educate us. Neither do the gossip "news about people" publications. But most of us still have the belief that we can trust what we see in the newspapers. Careful! The news media is quick to report as "news" an event that is out of the ordinary. They do not always verify their information.

The widely reported story of a man rendered unconscious by pressure applied into his armpits (by a woman he was attempting to assault) was hailed as a new and wonderful technique of self-defense. Nonsense.

Individuals who are assaultive are not in control of their emotions and are in a state of high anxiety. Breakdown, weeping, and running away are not uncommon reactions among assailants confronted with resistant behavior. The most likely explanation for the man's unconscious state is that he fainted.

HAND CONDITIONING IS NOT NECESSARY!

Hand conditioning, the hardening and callusing of the hands, is not appropriate for sport or self-defense karate or jujitsu; it is irrelevant to judo.

In sport karate, players do not make contact or they wear gloves.

In contest where contact is prohibited by the rules, players who have conditioned hands are required to wear bandages to minimize the possibility of injury if accidental contact is made.

In matches where contact is permitted, the players use padded gloves. A karate contestant who had spent years in hand conditioning would not be allowed to hit the opponent player with his hand weapon.

Sport judo rules forbid striking the opponent player with hand or foot blows.

For practical self-defense it is neither desirable nor necessary to condition your hands. Hand conditioning was an appropriate feature of ancient karate training. Because it was sometimes necessary to break through the wooden armor of the Samurai soldier, karate fighters in feudal times were required to spend years of effort to callus and desensitize their hands and feet so that they could deliver forceful blows to hard surfaces without feeling pain.

Today there is no reason to strike at hard surfaces in a manner which would hurt your normal, unconditioned hand. With an understanding of appropriate body target areas, you can avoid striking at hard, bony areas such as the collarbone (clavicle). When you do strike at a bony structure, such as the knee or the bridge of the nose, you can hit with appropriately forceful blows without hurting yourself. A kick into the knee does not require conditioning; hitting with the side of the closed fist onto the nose delivers enough force for self-defense use.

Heavy conditioning can cause permanent injury to your hands and it can seriously impair manual dexterity. Extreme hand conditioning is irreversible. The ability to do skillful, intricate work might be seriously reduced. If a job requires contact with the public, the misshapen appearance of conditioned hands could be an impediment to employment.

Heavy conditioning implies willingness to fight. Should you need to defend yourself on the street, you might have difficulty persuading the law that you were defending yourself; the evidence of conditioned hands would suggest preparation for fighting.

Hand conditioning is necessary if you want to do stunts and tricks such as breaking bricks without hurting yourself. If you really feel that it is important to show off in such a manner, you will have to work at long-term hand conditioning. Be aware that once you have heavily conditioned hands, you are risking the chance that they will never again be normal. It is a heavy price to pay for doing a stunt.

ACCURACY OF THE DESCRIPTIONS

It is my objective to be as accurate as possible in describing the effects of blows and techniques commonly used in self-defense and in sport fighting. There is a difference between accuracy for this purpose and exactness in the scientific sense.

To make a scientific evaluation of the effect and consequences of any particular technique (a hand blow, for example) it would be necessary to have the following information:

a. A precise measurement of the force of the blow.

b. An exact description of the area struck.

c. An exact measurement of the angle at which the blow was struck.

d. A complete description of the general health, past medical history and body structure of the person struck.

e. Professional medical examination of any injury, or, in the event of death, post-mortem examination and report.

f. To measure pain and emotional trauma one would have to know the state of mind and the general pain tolerance of the person struck.

It is clear that all of these complex factors cannot be examined to yield the information we want for our present purpose. Instead we must rely on the best available sources which come close to and are relevant to the subject. (In Nazi Germany doctors did pain-tolerance and injury experiments on healthy human beings. It is to be hoped that we will never see a repetition of this kind of "science.")

In the interest of achieving the degree of accuracy which is appropriate for this book there is frequent use of the words "possible" and "probable." They are used to remind you that exactness is not implied. "Possible" indicates that there is a chance the effect of the blow would produce the results described; "probable" indicates that there is a reasonable expectation that the blow would produce the results described.

The health and emotional state of the person being struck would modify the effect of the blow. The degree of force would modify the effect of a blow. The relative sizes of the people involved would be a modifying factor. For example, it is likely that a hand blow struck straight in at the solar plexus of a large person would yield the result of little pain and no other effect, but it would be inaccurate to say that such a result could be expected *under any circumstances.* If the large person being struck had an internal abnormality, weakness or disease and the person striking the blow had practiced to develop a fast punch which could deliver considerable force, the result could be serious.

COMPARING THE EFFECTS OF BLOWS

In considering the probable or possible effects of any particular blow, there are three situations to be considered: The opponents could be of approximately equal size and strength; the blow could be struck by a larger, stronger person against a smaller, slighter person; the blow could be used to defend against a larger, heavier assailant. There could be dramatic differences of effect in these different situations. Some examples follow.

1,2,3. In the three photos the identical open-hand slash is used and it is delivered to the identical target--onto the bridge of the nose.

1. The two people shown are about equal in size and build. The probable effects of this blow would be pain, possible bleeding and disorientation. Blurred vision might result temporarily. Permanent or serious injury is unlikely.

2. When the identical blow is delivered by a larger, heavier person against a smaller, lighter individual there is a greater possibility of serious or permanent injury. Because of the more favorable angle at which the blow is delivered to the target, because of the greater force delivered to the target and because of the presumably greater vulnerability of the person being struck, all of the effects described for photo 1 are present, but to a considerably greater degree. In addition there is a possibility of breaking the nasal bone and even the possibility of brain damage. Brain damage would not result from fracture of the nasal bone but from shock force of a blow to the head. A sufficiently forceful blow to any part of the head could cause brain damage.

3. A smaller, slighter person strikes the identical blow at a larger, heavier individual. The blow is the same as that shown in photos 1 and 2, but the small person hits at an awkward angle and would have difficulty reaching the target in the relationship illustrated here.

The probable effects of a full force blow in this instance would be quite different from the probable effects of the same blow illustrated in photo 2. Some pain might result but the likelihood of injury is remote.

1

2

3

4,5,6. In these photos the variants of size relationship, strength and the angle of the blow are shown for an open-hand slash into the side of the neck.

4. When opponents are of equal size and build the edge-of-hand blow struck into the side of the neck might stun and disorient. Depending on the force of the blow, there is a possibility of numbing the arm. A sufficiently forceful blow could cause unconsciousness and possible convulsions.

5. When the same blow is delivered at a smaller person by a larger adversary, there is greater probability of unconsciousness resulting. A sufficiently powerful blow could transmit shock force via the neck bones to result in brain damage and there is a possibility of irreversible damage to the carotid artery.

6. A forceful blow struck by the smaller individual against a heavier, stronger, larger adversary would result in pain and possible disorientation. The probability of injury is remote.

WEAPONS

The possible and probable effects of blows as they are described in this text refer to weaponless hand and foot blows. If a stick,bludgeon, baton, or any other weapon or implement were used the effects of the blow would be radically different. There would be a considerable increase in the degree of pain, the likelihood of injury, the seriousness of the injury and (if the blow were struck at a vulnerable area) a higher risk of fatality.

4

5

6

7,8,9. A knuckle blow is delivered to the solar plexus in three different situations.

7. As shown here with equal opponents, the probable effects would be pain, disorientation and gasping for breath.

8. Delivered at the angle shown and in the relationship of size and build illustrated, the probability of injury is dramatically increased. There could be referral shock to the spleen and to other vital internal organs.

9. When used by a smaller, slighter person against a heavier, stronger person, the identical blow has little effect.

7

8

9

10,11,12. Practical self-defense techniques are those which depend to the *least* degree upon relative power, size and build. Kicking into the knee or shin is an example of a highly practical self-defense action.

Though the effect would be different in different size relationships, the major advantage of this kick is shown in all three photos: The person kicking at the assailant does not have to come within fist or hand range of the assailant.

10. An adversary of approximately equal size is vulnerable to a kick into the knee or shin.

11. Kicking against a smaller person involves a considerably greater possibility of inflicting injury.

12. Although the probability of injury is considerably less when the same kick is delivered by a small person against a larger adversary, it is an effective technique for practical self-defense.

10

11

12

In contrast to the kick into the knee or shin, which can be effective for small or large people, the tactic shown in 13, 14 and 15 is virtually useless for a small person and is a high-risk-of-injury blow if applied by a strong, large person against someone slight or frail.

13. The fist or open-hand blow to the base of the neck could cause considerable pain if applied to an individual of approximately equal size and build. There is a possibility, though not great likelihood, of dislocating the seventh cervical vertebra, which is a serious injury.

14. The identical blow struck with force by a larger, stronger person against a smaller individual involves the probability of serious permanent injury.

15. Used by a small person against a larger assailant, it is unlikely that enough pain would result to make this action practical for self-defense.

MOVIE & TV FIGHT SCENES

Before the "karate or kung fu killer" had been discovered by filmmakers, it was the little judo expert who would creep up and drop the big guy with a judo chop to the back of the neck. It always worked in the movies because there was a stunt man paid to fall down. We rather suspected that was the case. Nowadays there are some actors who are highly skilled in the martial arts or who take special training for a fight scene, which makes it very difficult for the audience to distinguish reality from make-believe.

But no filmed fight scene is real regardless of the actor's fighting skill. Filmed fight scenes follow a written script which determines who shall win and who shall lose. The scene is choreographed and rehearsed over and over. It is shot many times to get the most dramatic effect. Sound effects, trampolines, stunt men reacting, special visual effects and camera angles--these and other film techniques are used to produce a spectacular fight scene.

— ALICE McGRATH

13

14

15

TEMPLE AREA. 16.

It is widely believed that the temple area is extremely vulnerable because of a mistaken notion that the skull is thinner and more fragile in this region. An examination of a skull in an anatomy class or in an anatomy textbook will confirm that the bone is as thick at the temple area as it is at several other places on the skull.

Vulnerability in the temple area is associated with the shape of the bone rather than its thickness. Because the skull is flat at the temple area referral shock to the brain is more intense than the referral shock of a blow to a curved skull area. If sufficient *force* is delivered, any type of blow to the temple area or any other part of the head could be fatal without fracturing the skull. Hemorrhage of blood vessels of the brain is the most common cause of death following a forceful blow to the head.

† Equal adversary: A moderate blow startles and stuns, and causes pain. With repeated blows to the head there is increased possibility of injury such as is sustained by some boxers whom we call "punch drunk." As noted above, any blow to the head, if sufficiently forceful, involves probability of brain injury.

† Against a smaller person: A moderate or heavy blow could result in unconsciousness or convulsions and there is the possibility of irreversible brain damage.

† Against a larger assailant: A moderate blow can startle and distract. A heavy blow could stun. Unless the larger assailant were peculiarly vulnerable, it is not likely that a small person would cause serious injury.

Blows which can be used are the heel-of-palm blow, the slash and the hammer blow. If an assailant is behind you, an elbow blow or slash can be used.

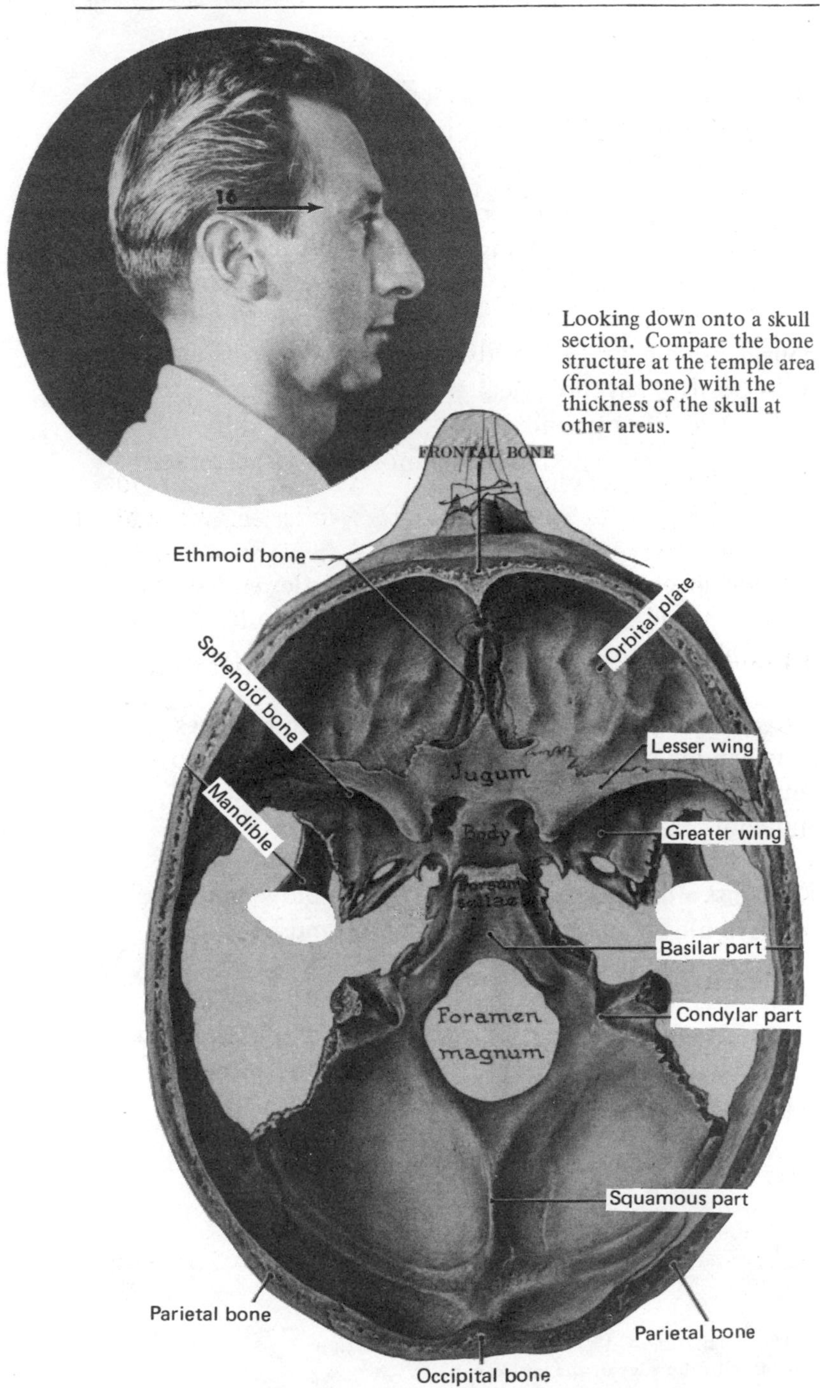

Looking down onto a skull section. Compare the bone structure at the temple area (frontal bone) with the thickness of the skull at other areas.

ONTO THE NOSE. 17.

If you are already in close to an assailant, this is an excellent target. DO NOT step in close to hit at the nose if you are out of fist-hitting range!

Hitting onto the nose is very likely to hurt, confuse and disorient an assailant. Drawing the head back and watering of the eyes are the two most common reactions to being hit on the nose. Even a moderate blow results in considerable pain. A bloody nose, while not serious, has a positive psychological effect in self-defense. Even when other possible targets are protected by clothing, an assailant's nose is almost always presented as an easy target.

† Equal adversary: A moderate blow startles and stuns; there is considerable pain; bleeding might result. A heavy blow could separate cartilage from the bone.

† Against a smaller person: A moderate blow causes considerable pain and disorientation. A forceful blow could result in separation of cartilage from the bone and could fracture the nasal bone.

† Against a larger assailant: A moderate blow causes pain. A heavy blow causes considerable pain and perhaps bleeding.

The most efficient hand blows onto the top of the nose are the hammer blow* and the edge-of-hand blow (also called slash, chop or knife-hand blow).

* The hammer blow is a closed-hand pounding action hitting with the edge of the curled hand.

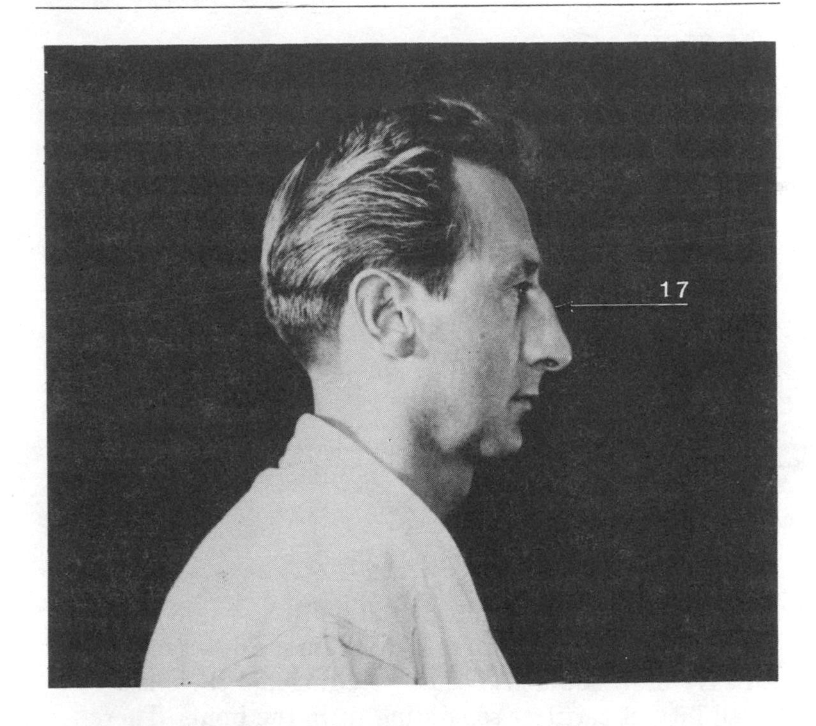

An open-hand slash onto the nose.

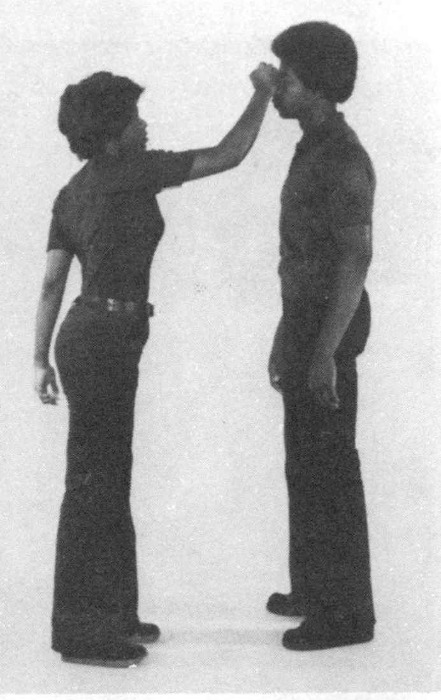

A closed-hand hammer blow onto the nose.

SIDE OF THE NOSE. 18.

Striking into the side of the nose is practical if the assailant is behind you.

† Equal adversary: A light blow distracts and usually results in a reflex action of pulling the head back. A moderate blow causes pain, might cause bleeding and there is a possibility of dislodging cartilage. A heavy blow would involve a possibility of nasal bone fracture in addition to the other effects just described.

† Against a smaller person: With a moderate or heavy blow there is considerable pain and disorientation, bleeding and the likelihood of dislocation of cartilage and/or bone fracture.

† Against a larger assailant: Striking into the side of the nose is distracting and there is momentary disorientation. A heavy blow could also cause bleeding and there is a possibility of cartilage separating from the bone. There is little likelihood of serious injury.

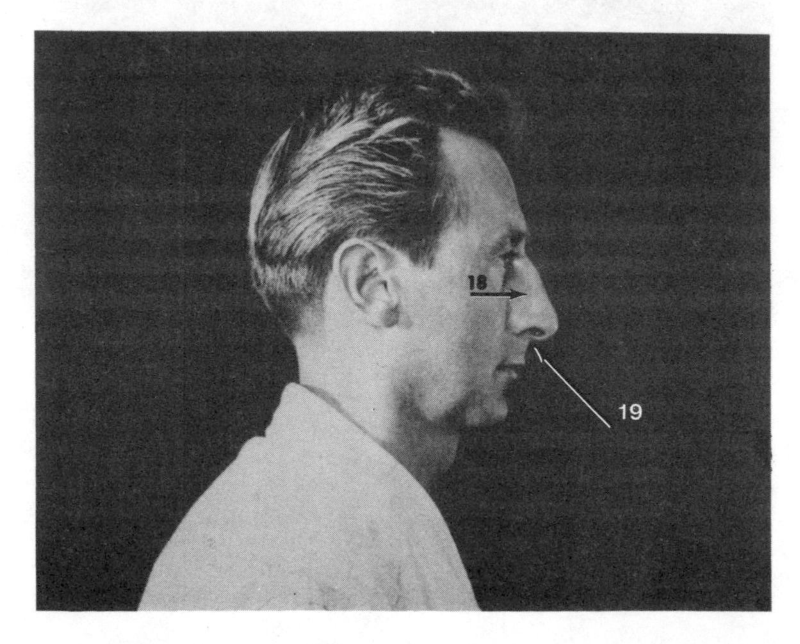

UP UNDER THE NOSE. 19.

This is an excellent target for a smaller person against a larger assailant, close in. Although it is widely believed that hitting up under the nose is a "deadly" blow, it is actually a low-risk-of-injury tactic.

† Equal adversary: A moderate blow causes pain and distraction; bleeding might result. A heavy blow might fracture the maxillary bone and/or cause cartilage separation from the bone.

† Against a smaller person: A moderate blow could cause bleeding and possible cartilage separation from the bone. A heavy blow could fracture the maxillary bone.

† Against a larger assailant: A moderate blow causes pain and momentary distraction. A heavy blow could cause bleeding. The likelihood of serious injury is remote.

From the front, the most effective blows up under the nose are the heel-of-palm blow or the slash. A slash can be used against an assailant from the rear; an elbow blow is effective, but requires greater precision than a slash blow.

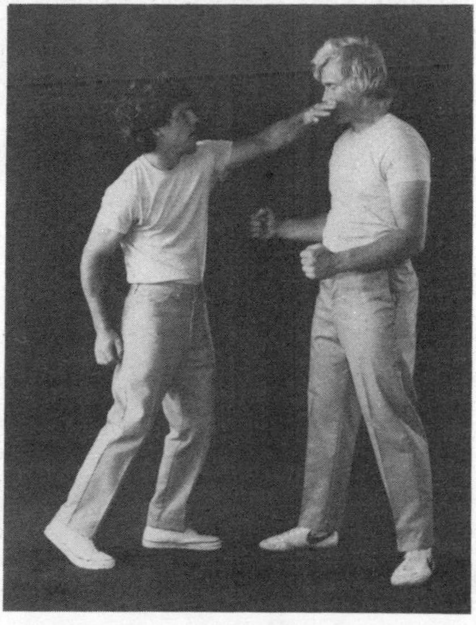

An open-hand slash up under the nose.

EYES. 20.

Striking into the eyes is a very high-risk-of-injury tactic. Its use would be justified only in the most serious kinds of assault. If your life is threatened, or extreme bodily harm is intended and if you are already close in there might be no practical alternative.

The slightest contact blow or fingernail scratch could result in serious and permanent eye injury. There is no justification for striking into the eyes if any other defense action would be effective. In some styles of kung fu training there is heavy emphasis on clawing and poking into the eyes. Such instruction is dangerously out of date; it does not take into consideration the legal, social or emotional consequences of inappropriately punitive responses to non-life-threatening assault.

† Because of the extreme delicacy and vulnerability of the eye, there is scarcely any difference in the effects of blows struck by a large or small person. Poking, clawing or stabbing into the eyes can cause permanent injury resulting in sight impairment or blindness.

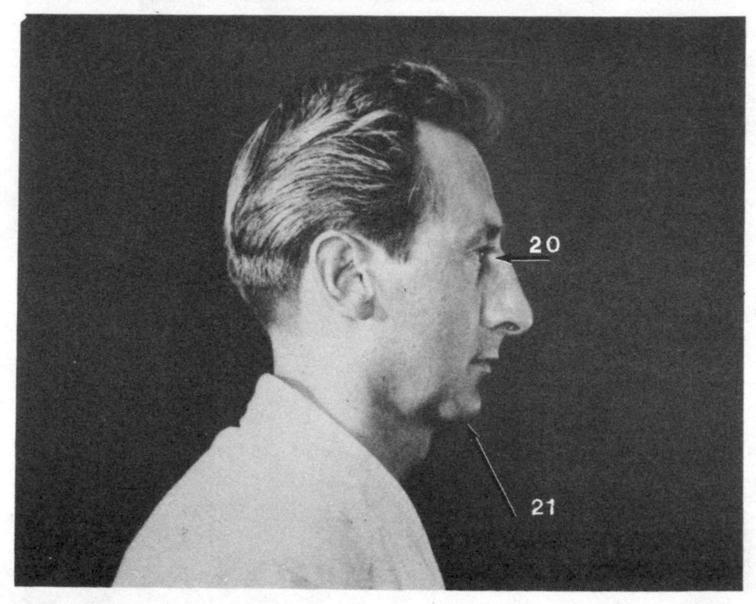

UP UNDER THE CHIN. 21.

This is an excellent target for practical defense and it is easily available to a smaller person already close in to a larger assailant.

† Equal adversary: A moderate blow snaps the head back and puts the assailant in an off balance position. A heavy blow could knock him unconscious. This is a classic boxer's knockout blow.

† Against a smaller person: A moderate blow could put him off balance, cause pain and jar the head. A heavy blow could result in unconsciousness. There is a possibility of bone or tooth injury.

† Against a larger assailant: A moderate blow jars the head and snaps it back. A heavy blow could put him off balance.

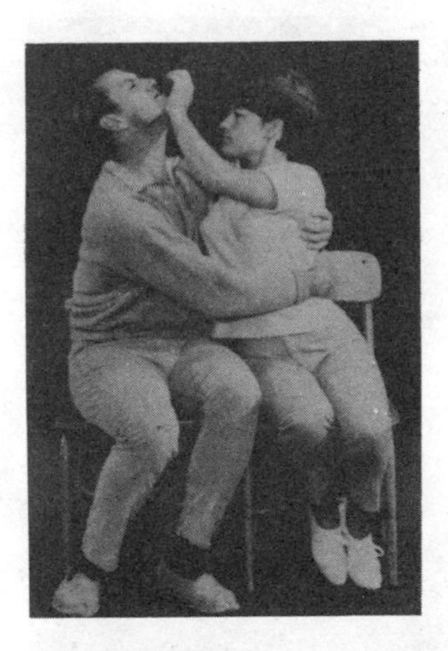

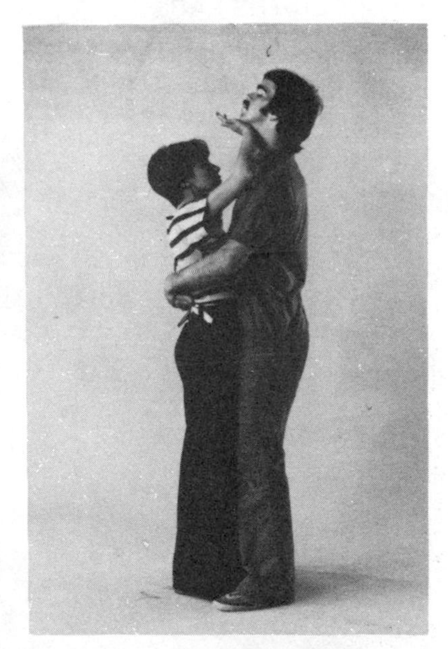

The heel-of-palm blow up under the chin can be used as a standing technique or from a seated position.

AT THE EAR. 22.

Blows to the ears are taught in many old-style martial arts. My objection to this target for modern self-defense is that it is not a practical striking area for a smaller person against a larger assailant and if it is used against a smaller person there is a possibility of hearing impairment.

†Equal adversary: A moderate blow can cause pain. A heavy blow might injure the inner ear.

† Against a smaller person: A moderate blow can jar the head and cause pain. A sufficiently forceful blow could cause hearing impairment or brain injury.

† Against a larger assailant: A moderate blow is not likely to be effective. A vigorous, cupped-hand blow could cause pain.

UP UNDER THE EAR. 23.

The hollow behind the ear is an area to which pressure can be applied to effect pain by grinding with the thumb or knuckle.

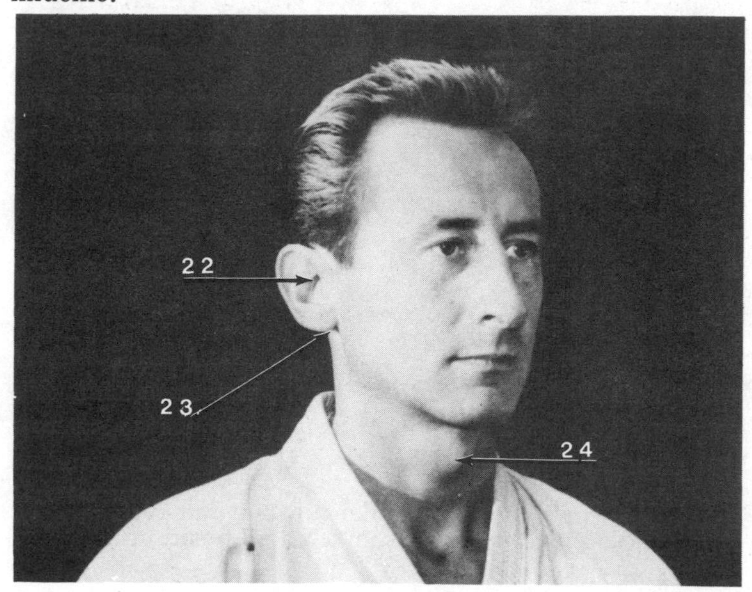

WINDPIPE/ADAM'S APPLE. 24.

Unless threatened with great bodily harm or vicious assault, striking into any portion of the windpipe (trachea) or onto the Adam's apple (thryoid cartilage) is neither justified nor appropriate. The area at the front of the throat is a most vulnerable, high-risk-of-injury target and should be avoided unless there is no practical available alternative.

† Equal adversary: Striking straight in with a moderate blow would result in pain, gasping and choking. There is a possibility of fatal injury.

† Against a smaller person: A moderate blow involves possibility of fatal injury; a heavy blow dramatically increases the likelihood of fatal injury.

† Against a larger assailant: A moderate blow could result in gasping and choking. A heavy blow could be fatal.

Against a vicious assault, and if you are already close in to the assailant, an edge-of-hand slash or a forearm blow could be used.

PRESSURE against any part of the windpipe (trachea) also involves risk of injury. Very slight pressure can cause pain. Heavy pressure against the trachea involves a high probability of fatality which could result from rupture of the trachea or from strangulation.

A person against whom a trachea pressure technique is applied is likely to struggle forward against the hold, thus increasing the force of the pressure. It is almost impossible for the person applying the hold to regulate the degree of pressure.

UP UNDER THE JAW. 25.

In this area there is a concentration of nerves. The target is behind and up under the jawbone. Except for the intensity of pain, there is no appreciable difference if this is done by a larger or smaller person. A jabbing or poking blow results in considerable pain. The extended knuckle or fingertips can be used.

THROAT HOLLOW. 26.

Below the thyroid cartilage there is a hollow where the windpipe (trachea) is least protected and most exposed. *Slight* pressure at the trachea in this area can be used to push an assailant away. Forceful blows into the throat hollow involve a high risk of serious injury.

Because of the vulnerability of the trachea, the result of light pressure against it will be much the same if done by a smaller or a larger person. Control of someone who is annoying or offensive but is not threatening great harm can be effected by placing the thumb into the hollow and applying slight pressure. Heavy pressure would involve probability of serious injury or fatality. Forceful knuckle jabs or finger stabs would have the same effect as striking into the thyroid cartilage.

Forceful blows, heavy pressure or vigorous stabbing into the throat hollow would be appropriate and justified only if great bodily harm were threatened.

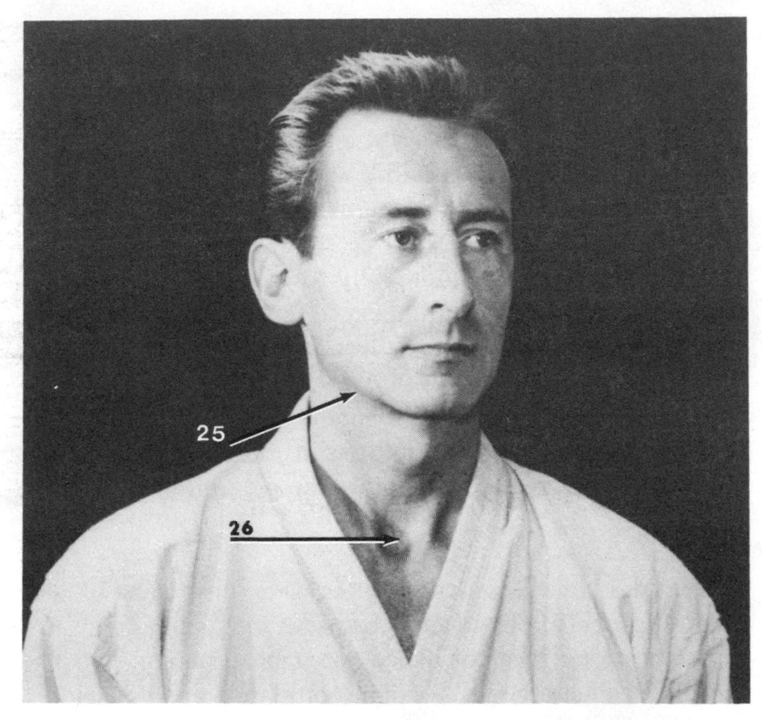

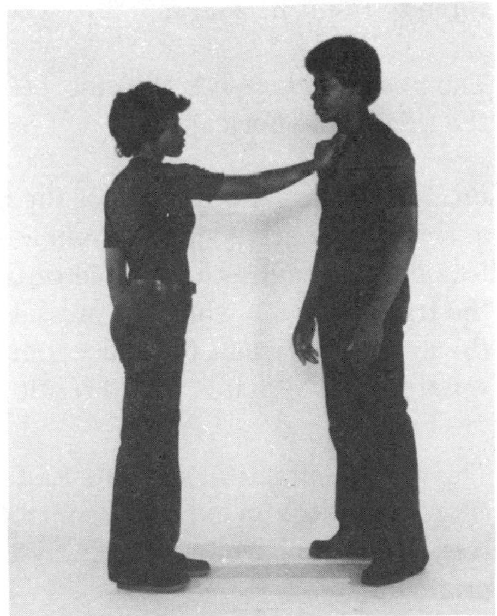

Slight fingertip pressure into the throat hollow.

SIDE OF THE NECK. 27.

This area includes the carotid artery and the jugular vein, and is an excellent practical self-defense target. It is sensitive to pain but it is not a high-risk-of-injury target unless a very forceful blow is struck or unless the person struck is particularly vulnerable--frail or ill.

† Equal adversary: A moderately forceful blow causes pain. A vigorous blow could cause temporary stunning. A very heavy blow could result in unconsciousness.

† Against a smaller person: A moderate blow could cause stunning. A heavy blow could result in unconsciousness and a very forceful blow involves the possibility of fatal injury.

† Against a larger assailant: A moderate blow causes pain. A forceful blow causes considerable pain and disorientation. It is not likely that a small person striking against a larger assailant could deliver sufficient force to result in injury.

The open-hand slash is the most efficient blow against the side of the neck.

PRESSURE against the side of the neck (a hold or bar at the carotid artery/jugular vein area) is considerably less likely to injure than a hold or bar applied against the trachea. Even when the pressure against the side of the neck is sufficient to render someone unconscious, it is not probable that it would result in irreparable or fatal injury.

This is not a practical self-defense technique for the lay citizen, but it is an excellent control tactic for professionals who have been properly trained in its appropriate use.

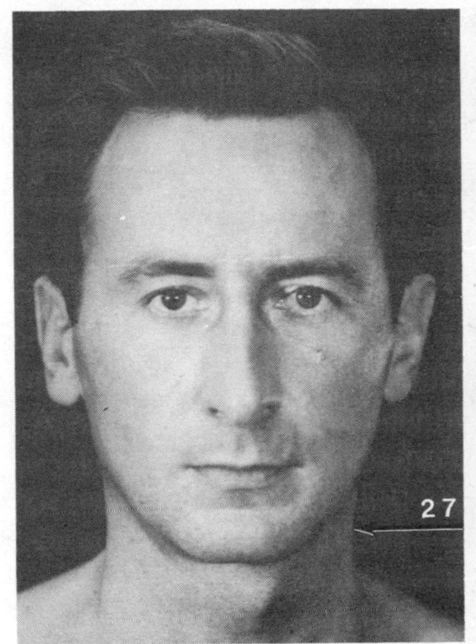

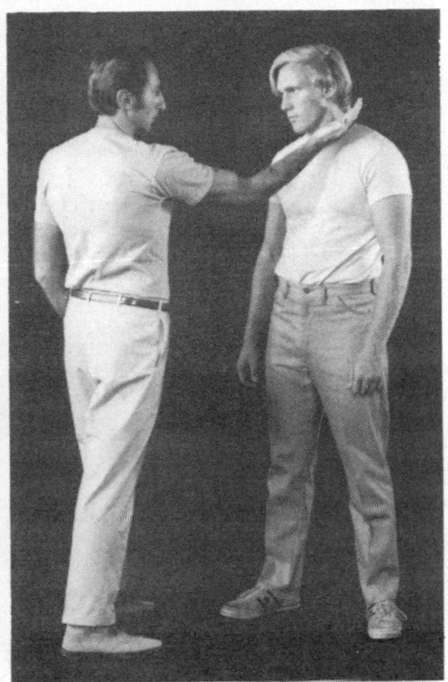

A slash into the side of the neck, delivered with the palm up.

A control hold applied against the side of the neck -- at the carotid artery.

There is a high risk of injury --*including fatal injury*-- if pressure is applied against the front of the throat at the thyroid cartilage and windpipe.

MUSCLE AT THE BASE OF THE NECK. 28.

Where the neck and shoulder join there is a muscle area which can present a practical self-defense target.

† Equal adversary: Striking down onto the muscle with a moderate blow causes pain. A forceful blow could numb the arm for a short time and it might result in muscle spasm, immobilizing the arm.

† Against a smaller person: A moderate blow causes considerable pain and could numb the arm. A forceful blow could result in a longer period of immobility and there is a possibility of muscle injury.

† Against a larger assailant: A moderate blow is ineffective. A forceful blow causes pain and could briefly incapacitate the arm.

The most practical blow is an open-hand slash.

COLLARBONE. 29.

This high ridge of bone is a favored target in old-style martial arts. Although fracturing the collarbone (clavicle) may be a disabling tactic which would be appropriate against a serious assault, I do not favor it for modern self-defense because it is hardly possible except for a larger person against a smaller individual or for those who have had considerable training and hand conditioning.

† Equal adversary: A moderate blow is ineffective. A forceful hammer blow could fracture the clavicle.

† Against a smaller person: A moderate blow is painful and jarring. A forceful hammer blow involves probability of fracture.

† Against a larger assailant: Little likelihood of appreciable effect.

A slash down onto the muscle at the base of the neck.

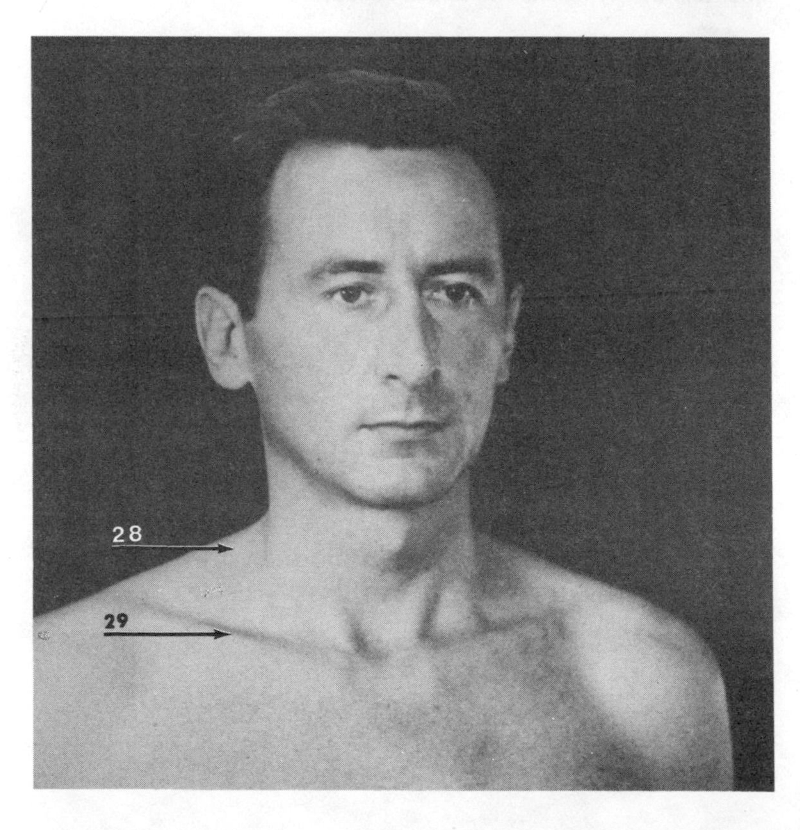

BASE OF THE SKULL. 30.

At the base of the skull is a target area of very limited use. Consisting of the first cervical vertebra and the second cervical vertebra, it is not practical for smaller individuals against a larger assailant as shown in photo 15. It is also a high-risk-of-injury target if used against a frail or small person by a powerful individual.

† Equal adversary: A moderate blow causes pain and possible headache. A sufficiently forceful blow could be fatal for one of two reasons: An extremely forceful blow directed upward against the target could refer fatal shock to the brain. Directed straight in at the target, a powerful blow could dislodge the first vertebra (the atlas) or fracture the second vertebra (the axis), either of which might result in permanent paralysis or fatality because of injury to the spinal cord.

† Against a smaller person: The probability of paralysis or fatality is increased if a power blow is directed against someone small or frail.

† Against a larger assailant: A moderate blow is ineffective. A forceful blow could cause pain or headache.

BASE OF THE NECK. 31.

A cliche of movie and television fight scenes is the judo chop, karate chop or rabbit punch to the base of the neck (seventh cervical vertebra). In films, the adversary goes down, no matter how big he is. In real life this does not happen.

For street defense this is not an appropriate target. A smaller person cannot use it effectively; if a larger individual strikes a power blow against a smaller person there is a high risk of injury.

To locate the target on your own self, drop your head forward and you can feel the prominent bone at the base of the back of your neck which is the seventh cervical vertebra.

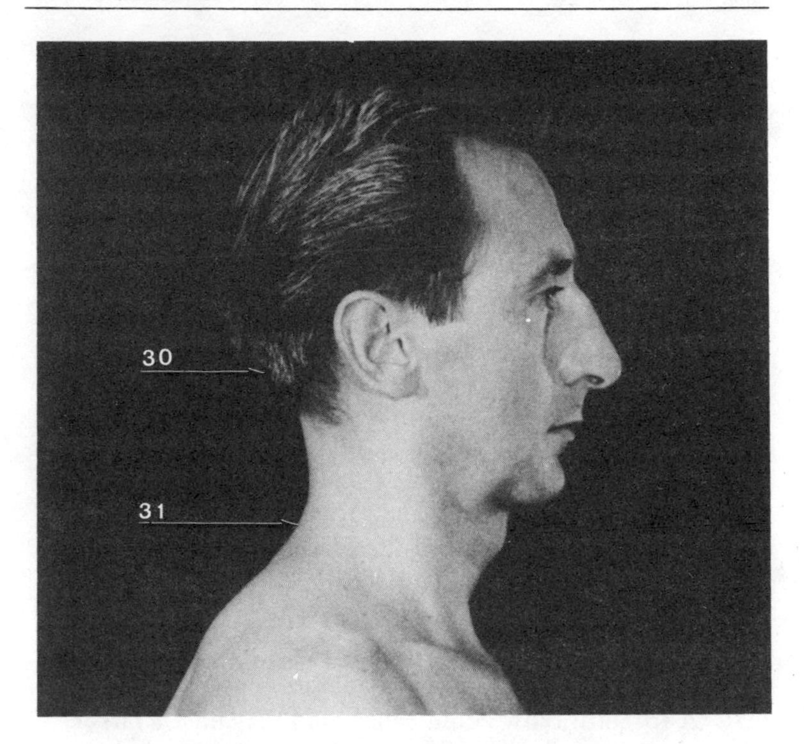

† Equal adversary: A moderate blow jars the body and causes pain. A forceful blow causes considerable pain and if it is sufficiently forceful there is a possibility of serious injury, paralysis or fatality.

† Against a smaller person: There is higher probability of serious injury, paralysis or fatality when a power blow is struck against a small or frail individual. Because of the angle at which a larger person is likely to strike at a smaller person, referral shock to the aortic arch is a possibility. The aortic arch is the major pathway for blood supply to the upper and lower parts of the body. If there is injury to the aortic arch, internal bleeding results and death is highly probable.

† Against a larger adversary: A moderate blow is ineffective. A forceful blow could cause pain.

BETWEEN THE SHOULDER BLADES. 32.

Slightly above and between the prominent bones of the shoulder blades is an area which is struck with the intention of referring shock force into the heart or the aortic arch and the vagus nerve. I do not favor this as a practical self-defense target. It is either high-risk (when a power blow is applied) or it is ineffectual, depending on the relative size and frame of the persons involved.

† Equal adversary: A moderate blow causes pain. A heavy blow could refer shock force into vital organs with a possibility of serious injury.

† Against a smaller person: The probability of serious internal injury increases with the force of the blow. Against a frail or slight individual this is a high-risk-of-injury area.

† Against a larger assailant: A moderate blow is ineffectual. A forceful blow could cause pain. Against a larger, heavier assailant the purpose of striking into this area would not be to effect pain but perhaps to push him off balance.

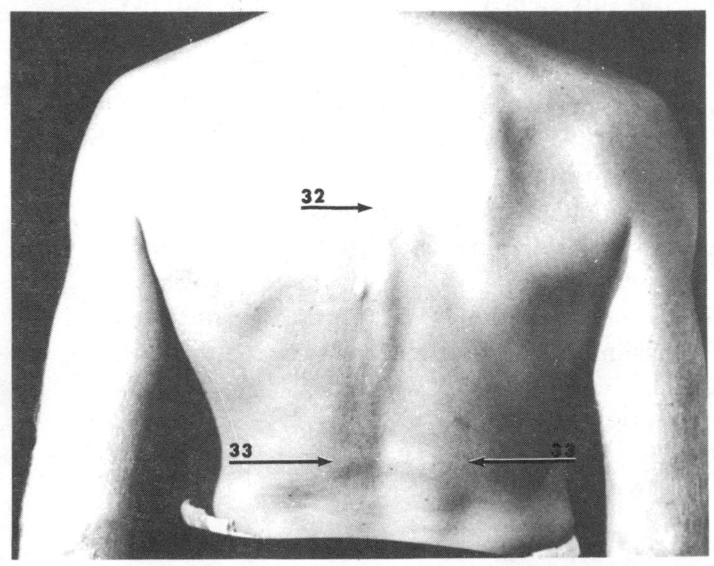

KIDNEY AREA. 33.

The kidneys are located at about the waist level, a few inches on either side of the spine. Approximately half of the kidney is protected by the lower ribs; the lower half is relatively unprotected, vulnerable and sensitive. If a power blow is delivered by a strong person there is high risk of serious internal injury.

† Equal adversary: A moderate hand blow is painful; there is slight possibility of internal injury. A heavy blow into the kidney area causes considerable pain and there is probability of internal injury. A sufficiently forceful blow could be fatal.

† Against a smaller person: Striking into the kidney area of a smaller person involves a risk of internal injury. The probability of delivering a fatal blow increases with the force of the blow and the relative sizes of the persons involved.

† Against a larger assailant: A moderate hand blow is unlikely to have an appreciable effect. A forceful hand blow could cause pain.

A hammer blow or elbow blow is used to strike into this area. In karate training, kicking into this area is commonly taught as a self-defense tactic. I do not favor this because of the high level of skill required and because the risk of injury from a kick is considerably more than from a hand blow.

† There is also a possibility of injury to the kidney by striking a forceful blow into the side; if the last rib is struck with sufficient force there is a possibility of a fractured rib rupturing the kidney.

SOLAR PLEXUS. 34.

This is not an anatomic entity, but is a term used to describe a striking area. It is the region below the breast bone, where the ribs part. There is a critical difference in the degree of pain, risk of injury and other effects depending on the angle of delivery of the blow as well as on the force of the blow and the health and frame of the individual being struck.

† Equal adversary: A moderate blow causes pain and could result in what is commonly called "knocking the wind out" which is in fact a temporary stoppage of breathing resulting from striking the diaphragm. A forceful blow could result in internal injury to the vital organs. A moderate blow struck in an upward direction causes considerable pain and sends referred shock to the vital organs with some possibility of internal injury. A forceful blow struck in an upward direction could cause serious permanent injury to one or more of the vital organs and there is a possibility of fatality.

† Against a smaller person: A straight-in moderate blow can interfere with breathing, is very painful and could stun. A forceful straight-in blow could result in unconsciousness and there is a probability of internal injury. A moderate blow struck in an upward direction involves possibility of internal injury. A heavy upward blow is a high-risk-of-injury tactic and the danger of fatality is increased by the force of the blow and the physical and emotional state of the person being struck.

† Against a larger adversary: Struck in an upward direction, a moderate hand blow can cause pain; a forceful hand blow could cause considerable pain and might briefly affect breathing. Unless the person being struck were particularly vulnerable because of illness or impairment, there is little likelihood that injury would result.

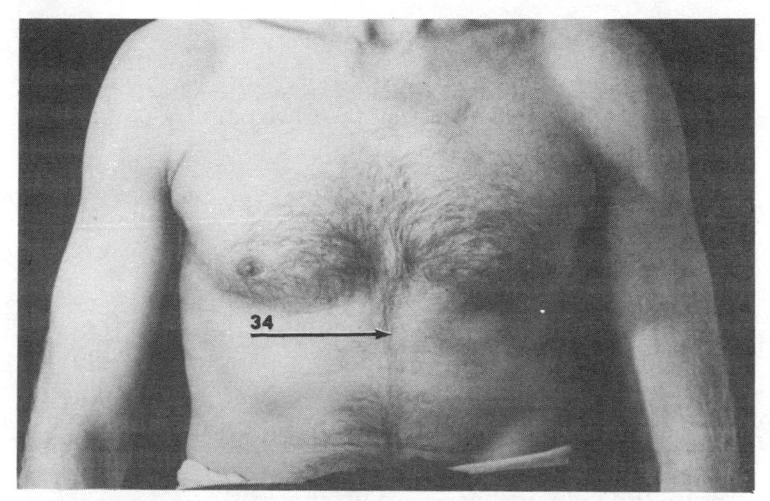

Straight-in blows are delivered with the fist or extended knuckle. An upward blow is delivered with the heel-of-palm or extended-knuckle blow. An elbow blow can be used to strike into the solar plexus region against an assailant standing behind you. A kick into the solar plexus delivers greater force than a forceful hand blow and because of the angle of delivery is more likely to cause severe injury.

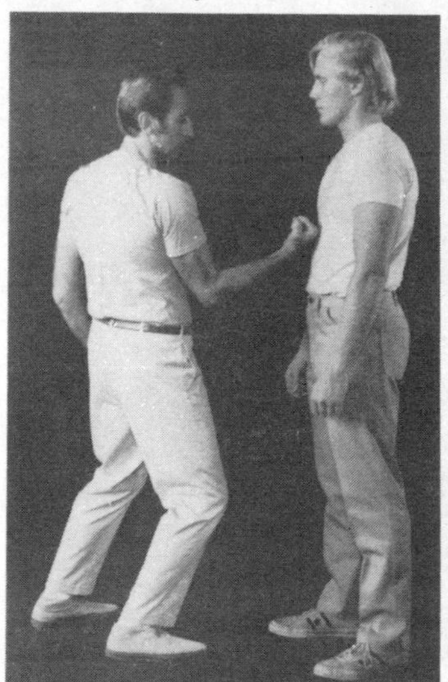

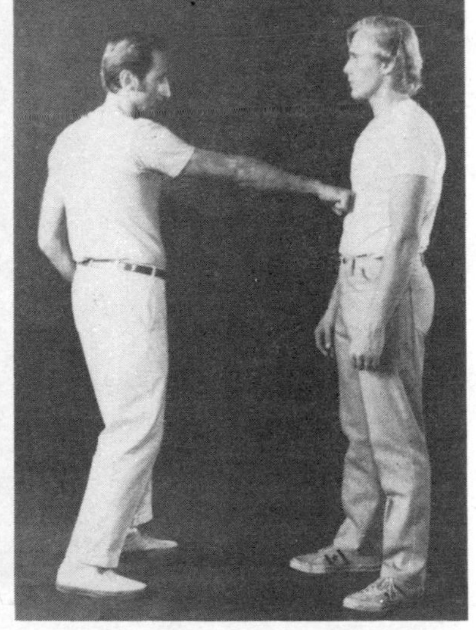

An upward blow (left) delivers far greater shock force to the internal organs than does a straight-in blow (right).

SIDE OF BODY, UNDER LAST RIB. 35.

This area is sensitive in a special way. Most people are ticklish here, but it is also easy to cause pain by jabbing directly below the last rib.

† Equal adversary: Digging with the extended knuckle or striking an open-hand blow would cause pain.

† Against a smaller person: A grinding action with the extended knuckle causes considerable pain with hardly any possibility of internal injury. A forceful hand blow or a kick might result in internal injury; if the last rib is struck with sufficient force it can fracture and might rupture the kidney--a very serious injury.

† Against a larger assailant: A digging action with an extended knuckle could be used to effect release from the grip of a larger person who is not threatening serious assault. It is unlikely that a smaller person could use a hand blow to this area with appreciable effect.

Digging into the side with knuckle extended -- it is a grinding action.

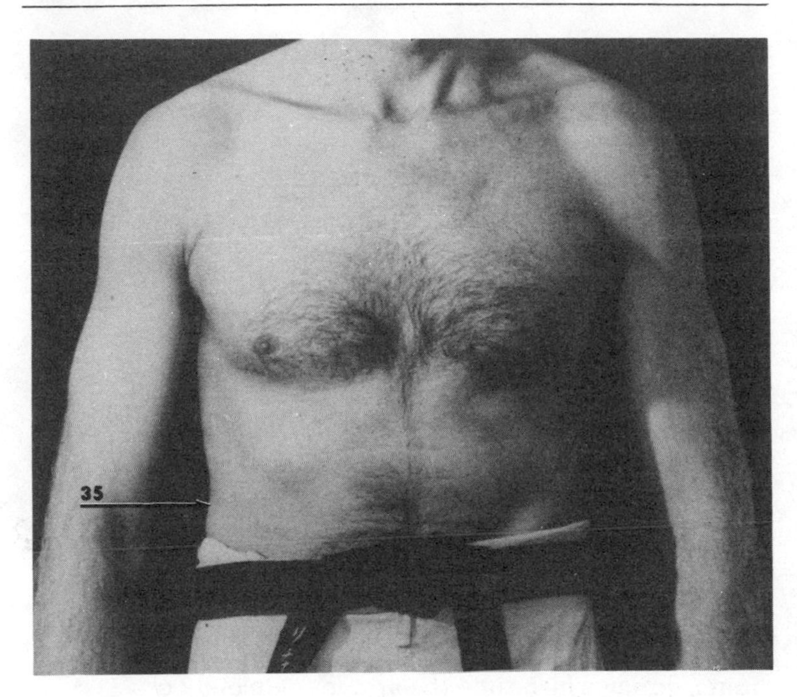
35

INSIDE OF ELBOW JOINT. 36.

Striking into the bend of the elbow causes pain and it bends the arm. This is a good striking point for practical self-defense; the smaller person need not come within the hitting range of the assailant in order to hit the target.

† Equal adversary: A moderate blow causes pain; a moderately forceful blow will bend the arm (or arms--simultaneous blows can be struck). A forceful blow will bend the arm and there can be a numbing effect which persists for a brief time. The numbing effect is similar to that which occurs when you hit the nerve at the back of the elbow joint (the funny bone).

† Against a smaller person: A moderate blow causes pain and can bend the arm (or arms). A forceful blow causes considerable pain, bends the arm and could result in numbness lasting from a few moments to as much as several hours, during which time the arm is completely or partially incapacitated.

† Against a larger assailant: A heavy blow into the elbow could bend the arm and cause pain.

The open-hand slash is the most effective hand blow into the bend of the elbow. A hammer blow could also be used.

OUTSIDE OF ELBOW JOINT. 37.

There is limited practical value to the tactic of striking at the back of the elbow joint. In some circumstances, the arm may be extended in such a way that the back of the elbow presents itself as a target. It can be struck to effect pain or it can be struck with force to incapacitate the arm.

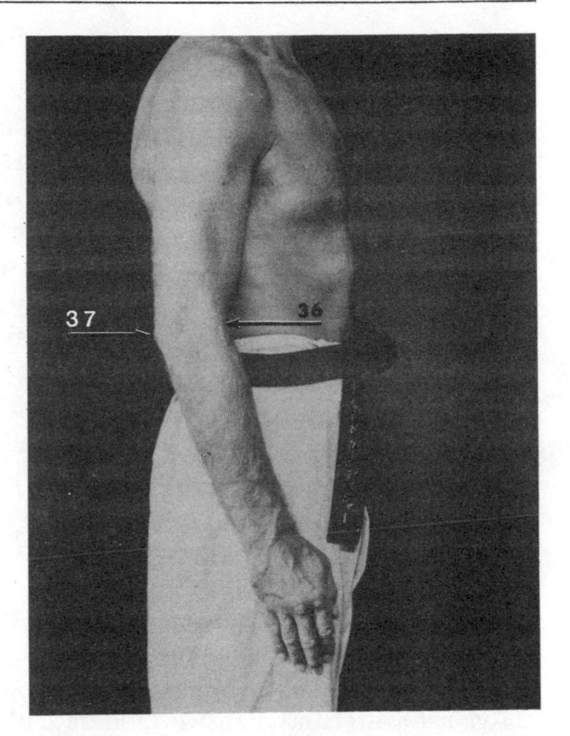

† Equal adversary: A moderate blow causes pain. A forceful blow could cause extreme hyperextension and could injure or tear cartilage, incapacitating the arm. Surgery is required to restore cartilage and muscle function unless the injury is slight.

† Against a smaller person: The probability of injury to muscle and cartilage increases dramatically when a forceful blow is applied against a smaller person. Moderate pressure against the elbow joint to hyperextend it might be a suitable control tactic for a law enforcement officer.

† Against a larger assailant: A moderate blow would have little appreciable effect. A forceful blow could cause pain and might numb the arm briefly.

A forearm blow is most efficient. A hammer blow could be used but would require greater precision.

FOREARM MOUND. 38.

Just beyond the elbow is an area which, on most people, is very sensitive to pain. If you extend your arm you can see the top of the mound, which is the target area. Using a hand blow onto the forearm mound, it is not necessary to hit with precision. A blow aimed at the mound will refer force into the sensitive area. If you press your thumb into your own arm at this point you will discover how little pressure is needed to effect pain.

† Equal adversary: A moderate blow causes pain. A forceful blow causes considerable pain and can numb the arm.

† Against a smaller person: A moderate blow causes considerable pain and possible numbness. A forceful blow can numb and partially incapacitate the arm for from a few minutes to as much as an hour.

† Against a larger assailant: A moderate blow causes slight pain and distraction. A forceful blow causes considerable pain and can numb the arm briefly.

The most effective blow is the open-hand slash.

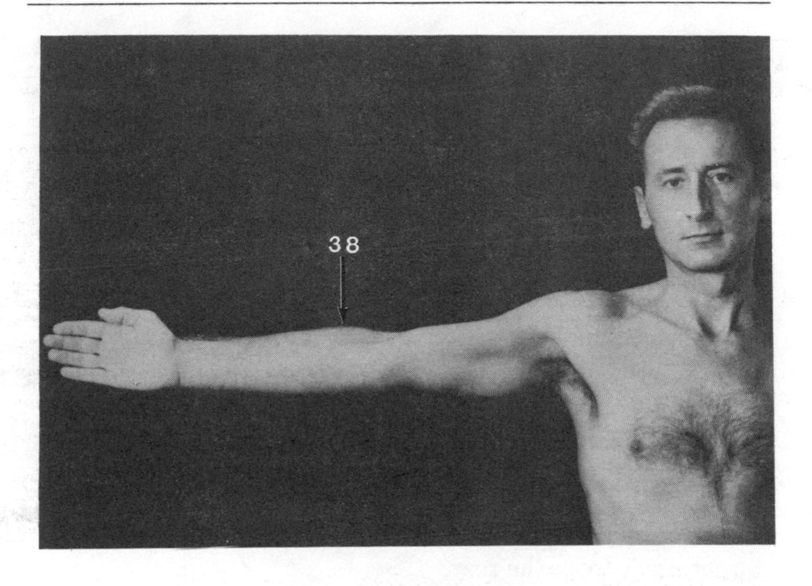

An open-hand slash is used to hit the forearm mound.

WRIST. 39.

Striking at the wrist is principally used as a deflecting action. Although a smaller person cannot easily block a larger assailant's arm, hitting the wrist with a sharp, slashing blow can deflect a reaching or grabbing attempt.

† Equal adversary: Deflection.

† Against a smaller person: A heavy blow could cause bone injury.

† Against a larger assailant: Deflection.

40, 41. The forearm mound and the wrist can also be target areas from the rear.

BACK OF UPPER ARM. 42.

At the back of the arm, midway between the elbow and shoulder, is a sensitive area.

† Equal adversary: A moderate blow has little effect. A forceful blow causes pain and possible numbness.

† Against a smaller person: A moderate blow causes pain and could numb the arm. A forceful blow causes considerable pain and could cause muscle spasm.

† Against a larger adversary. A heavy blow would cause some pain, but this is not a particularly good target for a smaller person against a larger assailant.

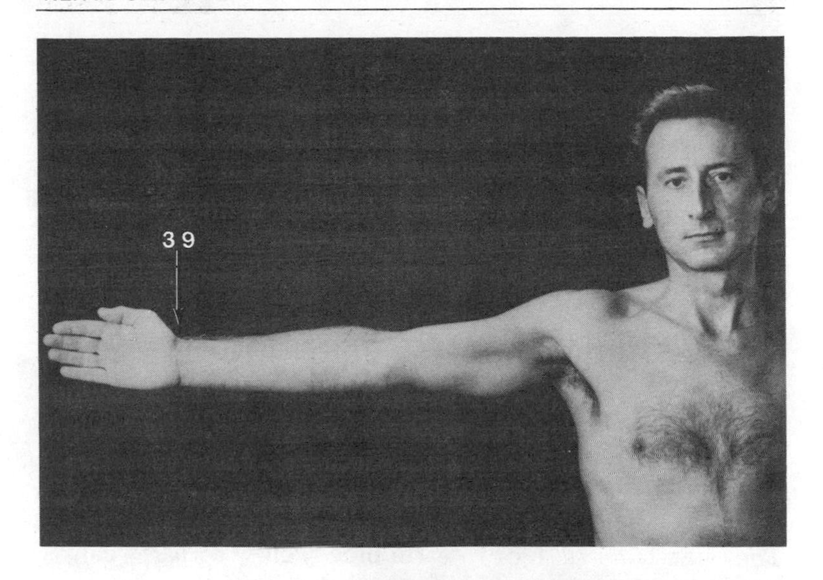
39

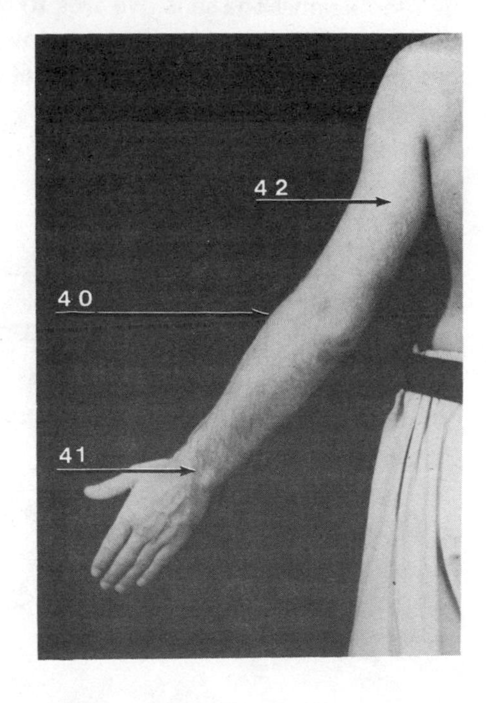
42
40
41

LOWER FOREARM. 43.

About two inches above the wrist on the thumb side of the forearm there is a sensitive area.

† Equal adversary: A moderate blow is somewhat painful. A forceful blow causes considerable pain.

† Against a smaller person: A moderate blow is painful. A forceful blow causes considerable pain and might result in a bone bruise.

† Against a larger assailant: A moderate blow is ineffectual. A forceful blow is painful.

The open-hand slash or forearm block, blow or parry can be used against the sensitive area to deflect and to cause distracting pain. Or, as shown below, the outer forearm can be the target for a deflecting action.

A forearm block against the forearm.

BACK OF THE HAND. 44.

The back of the hand is sensitive between the tendons and bones. A grinding or digging action is used.

† Regardless of the relative size of the people, digging into the back of the hand with an extended knuckle is likely to be quite painful.

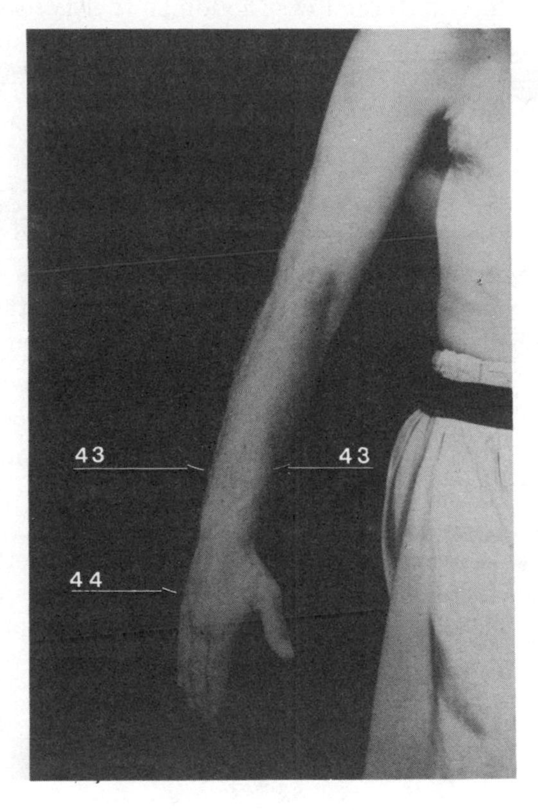

LOWER ABDOMINAL AREA. 45.

As has been noted repeatedly, the effect of any blow is modified by the factors of force delivered to the target area, general health and build of the person being struck, the angle at which the blow is delivered and the emotional and physical stance of the person being hit. These complex factors are particularly critical with respect to a blow into the lower abdomen (pelvic region). From the front, the bladder and lower intestines are unprotected by bony structure; in women the reproductive organs are vulnerable.

I view this as an inappropriate target for general self-defense. The degree of force necessary to effect pain carries with it a high risk of injury to vital organs.

A smaller person cannot strike into this area with much likelihood of appreciable effect unless the smaller individual is highly trained and can deliver a powerful blow.

† Equal adversary: A moderate hand blow causes pain. A forceful blow causes considerable pain and there is a possibility of internal injury.

† Against a smaller person: A moderate blow is painful and might cause internal injury. With a forceful blow there is considerable risk of injury to the internal organs.

† Against a larger assailant: A moderate hand blow is unlikely to produce appreciable effect. A forceful blow could cause considerable pain. There is a possibility of injury if a kick is used.

GROIN. 46.

Although hitting and kicking into the groin is a classic technique of old-style self-defense and grabbing the testicles is often taught for women's self-defense, I do not favor this area as a target. A blow or kick into the groin is excruciatingly painful, but it is an almost automatic reaction for men to protect the groin.

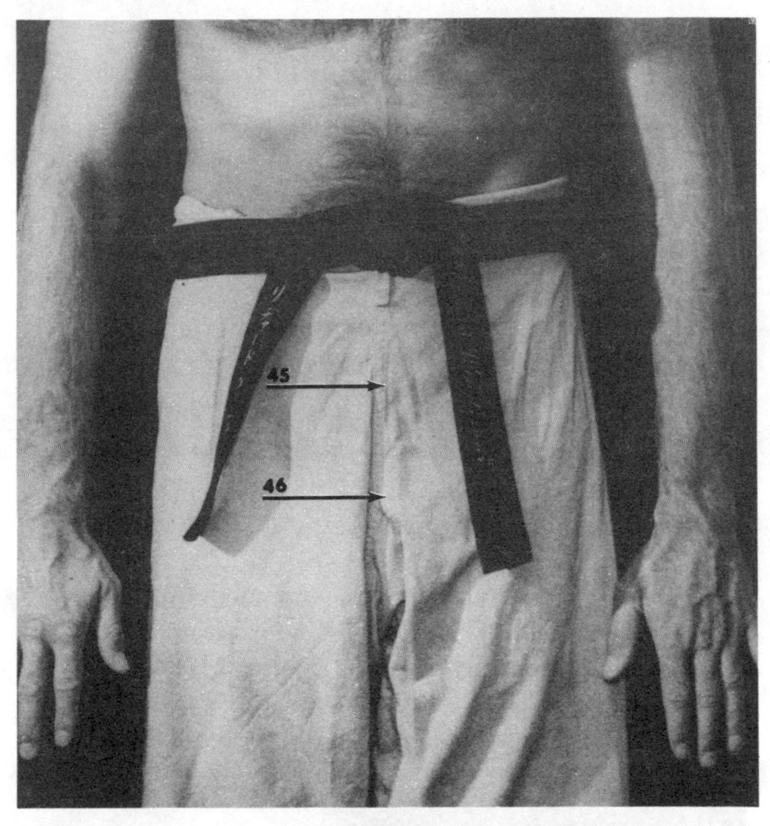

In many instances of assault the groin is not available as a target area. It is necessary to come in very close in order to use a knee kick to the groin; unless you are already in close, it is unwise to move into hitting distance. There is a strong element of sexual counterviolence in the use of this tactic and many people are reluctant to use it for this reason.

Violent, assaultive individuals and punitive persons are likely to recommend groin blows even when less repugnant defense tactics would be effective and appropriate.

In those situations in which a blow to the groin would be appropriate, a knee kick is used close in. Where an extended-leg (ball of foot or stamping) kick could be used, I would strongly recommend the knee as an alternative target.

UPPER INNER THIGH. 47.

Along the inner thigh, extending about halfway down to the knee, there is a very sensitive area.

† Equal adversary: A moderate, penetrating blow causes pain. A forceful blow causes considerable pain and could numb the leg.

† Against a smaller person: Moderate pressure is painful; a moderate blow could be very painful and a forceful blow is likely to numb the leg.

† Against a larger assailant: A moderate hand blow would have little effect. A forceful hand blow or a kick can cause considerable pain.

To deliver a penetrating blow, the extended-knuckle hand blow or an elbow blow would be practical. A toe kick would deliver penetrating force, but it is not a first-choice practical self-defense tactic.

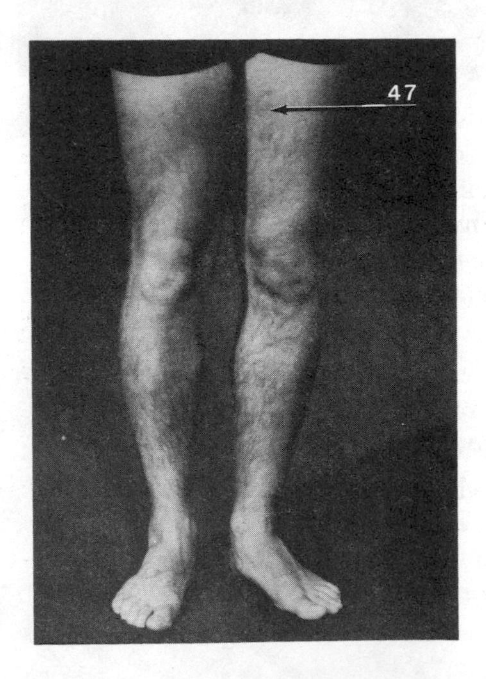

KNEE. 48, 49.

The knee is a prime self-defense target area. It is vulnerable. It can be reached (by kicking) from out of range of an assailant's fists. It can be used close in. It can be used as a target from almost any angle and it is available as an effective target for small individuals defending against considerably larger assailants. Although injury is a possible result, a knee injury is not life-threatening.

The angle of the kick will affect the result. A kick into the side of the knee is likely to unbalance or put an assailant onto the ground. A kick into the front of the knee is less likely to unbalance, but more likely to injure ligaments and/or dislocate the kneecap (patella).

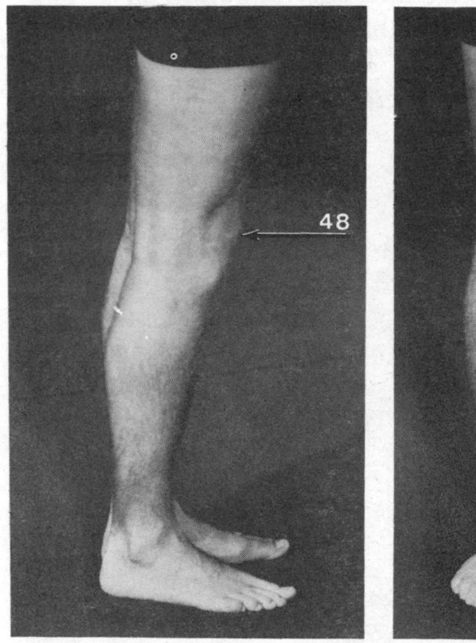

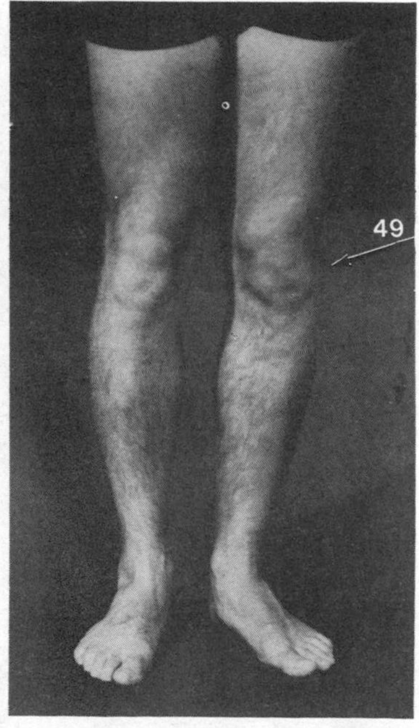

A kick made straight in at the knee, as shown in 48 is more likely to cause injury. Delivered at an angle into the side of the knee, 49, the kick is more likely to unbalance.

† Equal adversary: A moderate kick at a 45-degree angle (approximately) into the side of the knee is likely to cause loss of balance and pain. A forceful kick could tear or rupture the ligaments and/or tear cartilage. Dislocation of the kneecap is possible. Kicking straight into the front of the knee with force can result in severe hyperextension and serious injury to ligaments, cartilage and patella.

† Against a smaller person: A person of slight build is not more likely to be injured because of a kick to the knee due to the greater probability of being put on the ground rather than absorbing the impact in place. A smaller individual held immobile and kicked into the knee would, of course, be in greater danger of serious and severe injury. A moderate kick could result in injury to ligaments, cartilage and possible dislocation of the patella, if delivered at an approximately 45-degree angle. A frontal kick of moderate or greater force could severely hyperextend the knee, resulting in injury to the ligaments and cartilage and dislocating the patella.

† Against a larger assailant: A forceful kick at a 45-degree angle can buckle the knee and put a larger person off balance. There is a possibility of tearing ligaments or cartilage. A forceful kick into the front of the knee could tear ligaments and cartilage and there is a possibility of dislocating the patella.

A kick into the knee.

A long-range kick into the knee, safely out of range of the assailant's arm reach.

BACK OF THE KNEE. 50.

† A kick into the back of the knee, unless the leg is braced and unable to give with the blow, is most likely to result in buckling the knee and putting the individual onto the ground. Against a rigid knee, a kick from the back could injure cartilage and tendons.

From any angle, a stamping kick into the side, front or back of the knee is the most efficient technique.

Kicking into the back of the knee.

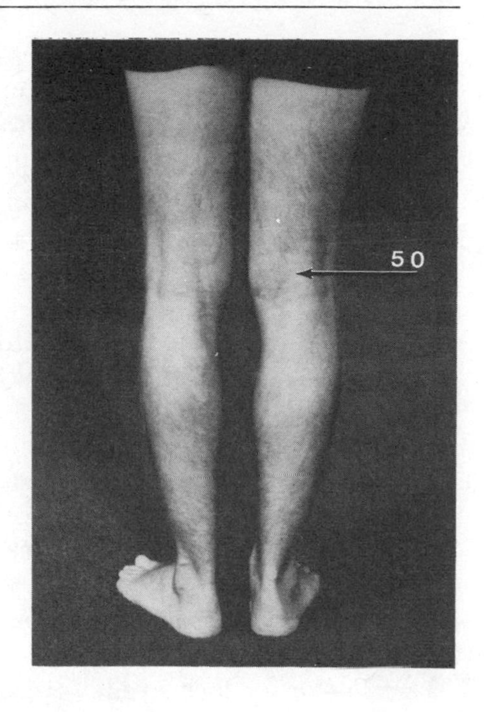
50

SHIN. 51.

On most people the shin area is peculiarly vulnerable to pain. It is possible to bring about pain by merely pressing onto this area and most of you will recall intense pain resulting from accidentally bumping the shin. This is an excellent self-defense target and particularly useful for a smaller person defending against a larger assailant.

† Equal adversary: Moderate kicking blows result in extreme pain. A forceful blow may involve a possibility of fracture.

† Against a smaller person: A moderate kick results in excruciating pain and there is a possibility of bone bruise. A sufficiently forceful kick could fracture.

† Against a larger assailant: A moderate blow causes pain. A forceful kick is very painful. It is unlikely that a smaller person kicking a larger assailant would cause greater injury than a bone bruise.

The most effective kick into the shin is made with the edge of the foot or shoe; the thin edge of the kicking surface results in penetration of force.

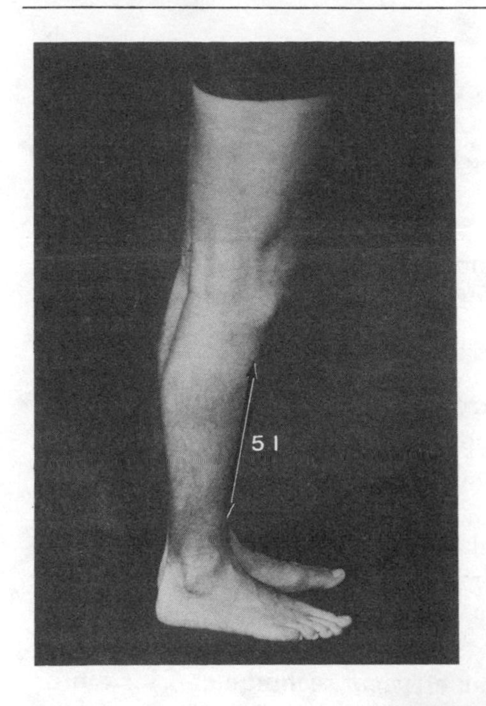

An edge-of-shoe kick into the shin.

INSTEP. 52.

The arched upper area of the foot is vulnerable to pain. There are many small bones in the foot; a blow of sufficient force to cause fracture could fracture more than one bone.

† Equal adversary: A moderate stamping blow causes considerable pain. A forceful blow could result in bone fracture(s).

† Against a smaller person: A moderate blow is extremely painful and there is a possibility of fracture. A forceful stamping involves probability of fracture(s).

† Against a larger assailant: A forceful blow causes pain; against a larger, heavier person there is no great likelihood of fracture.

The stamping blow is an efficient technique. A kick into the shin, followed by a scraping down the shin and completed with a stamping onto the instep is a particularly effective defense combination.

A kick into the shin is followed through with a scrape down the shin and a stamp onto the instep.

ANKLE. 53.

The ankle region is vulnerable to pain. It is also particularly susceptible to sprain.

† Equal adversary: A moderate or forceful kick results in considerable pain. Fracture or sprain could result from a kick of sufficient force.

† Against a smaller person: A moderate blow causes considerable pain. A forceful kick could result in fracture or sprain, or both.

† Against a larger assailant: A moderate kick would result in some pain. A forceful kick could cause considerable pain with a possibility of sprain. It is not likely that a smaller person could deliver sufficient force to cause fracture.

To cause pain, the edge-of-shoe snap kick would be most effective. Used with sufficient force a snap kick could cause fracture. A stamping kick could also be used to strike the ankle target.

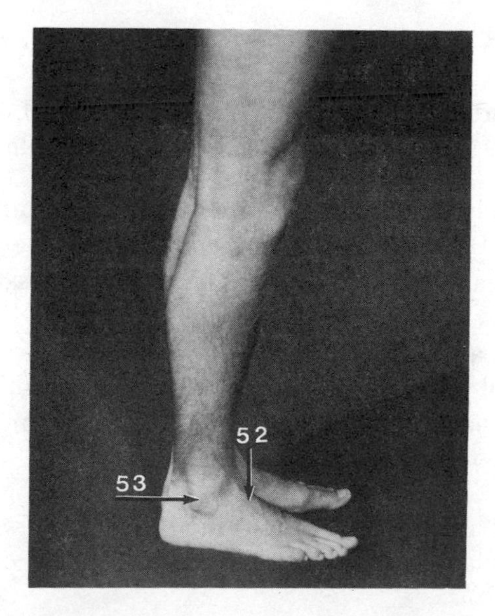

COCCYX. 54.

Commonly called the tailbone, this is the extremity of the spinal column. I do not favor this as a target area for practical self-defense. Perfect accuracy and considerable power are needed to deliver effective blows, which makes it a poor target for most people. If precision power blows are delivered to this area, there is a high risk of severe injury.

† Equal adversary: A moderate blow has little effect. A forceful blow causes considerable pain; a sufficiently powerful blow could result in severe injury.

† Against a smaller person: A moderate blow is painful. A forceful blow could cause internal injury, including damage to the spinal column and the spinal cord, with high risk of serious, irreversible injury.

† Against a larger assailant: A moderate blow has little effect. A forceful blow could cause pain.

A knee or toe kick is used to hit into this area.

BACK OF THE THIGH. 55.

A blow struck into this area is effective only if delivered with force -- using a stamping kick, for example.

† Equal adversary: A moderate blow causes some pain. A forceful blow is painful and could bring on a muscle spasm (charley horse) which is temporarily disabling.

† Against a smaller person: A moderate blow causes pain. A forceful blow is likely to cause muscle spasm with considerable pain. The probability of injury is minimal unless great force is used.

† Against a larger assailant: A moderate blow would have no appreciable effect. A forceful blow would cause some pain.

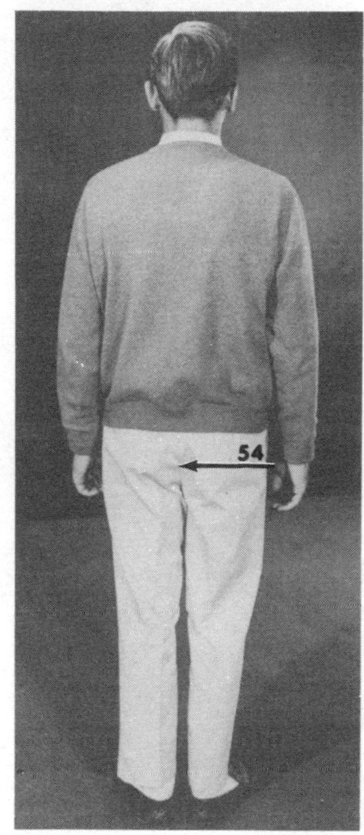
54

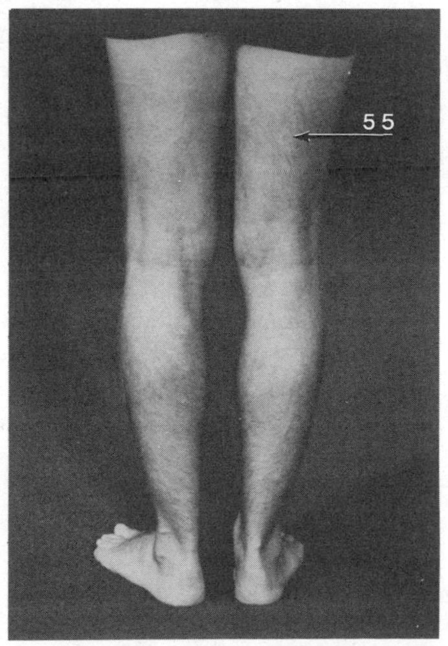
55

CALF. 56.

The fleshy area of the back of the leg just below the knee is a target for foot blows.

† Equal adversary: A moderate kick causes pain. A forceful kick would cause considerable pain and perhaps result in muscle spasm.

† Against a smaller person: A moderate blow causes considerable pain. A forceful blow might cause muscle spasm and considerable pain.

† Against a larger assailant: A moderate kick causes pain. A forceful kick would cause considerable pain.

The stamping kick or toe kick could be used.

ACHILLES TENDON. 57.

The long tendon which extends from the calf muscles to the heel bone is prominent and most sensitive at its lower extremity.

† Equal adversary: A moderate kick causes pain. A forceful kick would cause considerable pain with a possibility of injury to the tendon.

† Against a smaller person: A moderate blow causes considerable pain. A forceful blow could cause painful injury to the tendon or tear it.

† Against a larger assailant: A moderate kick is somewhat painful. A forceful kick causes considerable pain.

The edge-of-shoe kick is the most efficient technique; a stamping kick could also be used.

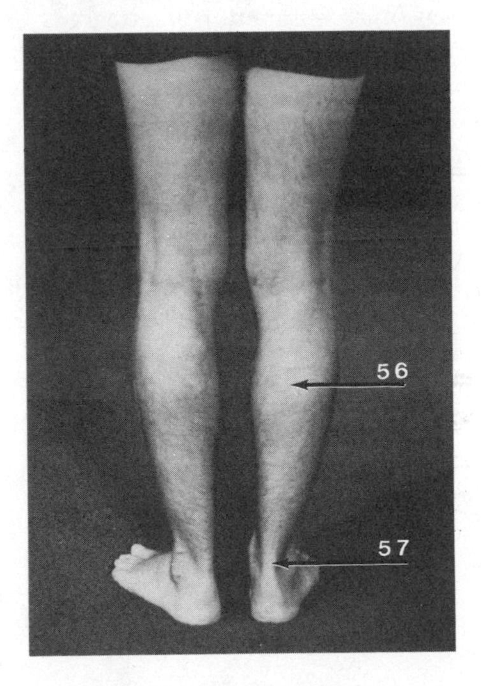

SUPPLEMENT

LOCATING THE TARGET

Depending on the season, the weather and the style of clothing, there are some target areas which would be somewhat protected, some target areas which would be altogether protected and concealed by clothing, and some which are likely to be exposed no matter what type of clothing is worn.

58. This illustrates the revealing/concealing characteristics of casual dress.

The head is exposed, as are the neck, wrists and hands. The casual shoes leave the ankle and instep exposed and available.

Other target areas would have to be gauged approximately. For this reason target points which require absolute precision to hit are not practical for basic self-defense for most people in most situations. The target areas which are practical for self-defense can be hit even when covered by clothing.

To hit the forearm nerve center, aim slightly below the elbow; the elbow joint is clearly visible in light clothing.

The knee, which is an excellent target for defense in serious assault, can be struck with reasonable accuracy even when covered. The shin can be struck at any point from the knee to the ankle.

In this type of clothing the solar plexus region can be located without difficulty. A blow struck slightly below the target is more effective than a blow struck too high.

58

In heavier clothing a scarf, collar or sweater might protect the neck, eliminating the side of the neck as an available target, but the nose is almost always exposed.

The shin can be struck through fairly heavy clothing; high-top boots would eliminate the shin as a target. Thick or high-top shoes would protect the ankle and instep.

Against vicious, life-threatening assault, the throat and eyes are ordinarily available as target areas. If the assailant were wearing glasses, the glasses could be knocked off as part of the defense action. Individuals who wear glasses regularly are handicapped and disoriented by their loss.

59. From the side, targets which might be available could be the head and neck, the forearm, knee and ankle.

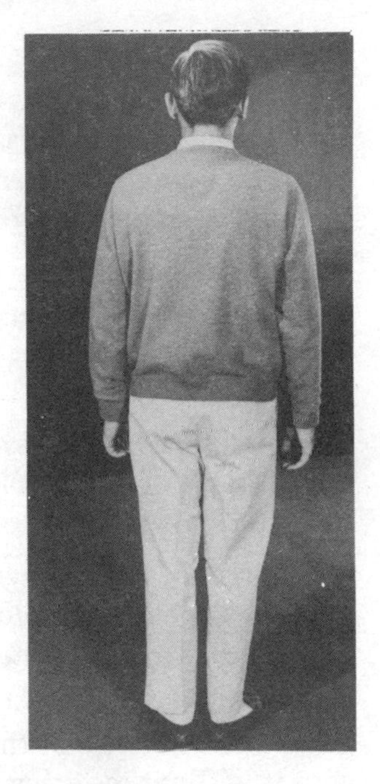

60. From the back, the side of the neck could be a target unless it is protected by thick clothing. The back of the knee is the best and most easily available target from this angle. It is easy to see the wrinkles and creases which show where the knee hinges.

"BEST" TARGET AREAS

There are no "best" targets in an absolute sense. There are different best targets for different situations. What might be a good target area in one instance might be impractical, impossible or inappropriate in another.

It would be practical to parry or strike at the arms in response to the reaching action shown in photo 61, but clearly inappropriate for the situation illustrated in photo 62.

The defense action in response to the threat of assault shown in photo 63 would not be possible in the situation shown in photo 64.

A high-risk-of-injury target such as the eye would not be the best target for a mildly offensive action but it would be the best target in a life-threatening situation.

Ethical self-defense involves judgment of the degree of danger and a choice of the appropriate tactic to deal with it without resorting to needless violence.

61

62

63

64

ACCURACY & SPEED PRACTICE PROCEDURES

The most common assault situations involve a smaller person defending against a larger or stronger assailant. For this reason you cannot rely on power blows unless you spend a great deal of time training and practicing to develop power.

For most people it is more realistic and sensible to learn how to make appropriate, prompt responses to the *threat* of assault and to learn the appropriate targets for hand and foot blows delivered with reasonable accuracy and speed.

Look at the target. Although this may seem to be superfluous advice, it is very important. It is common for most of us to look at objects without concentration. It takes conscious effort to keep your eye on the target.

Practice by looking at objects to register fully their shape, color, texture and mass. If you concentrate on the *act of looking* it will help you develop precision in hitting the target.

HITTING A SMALL MOVING OBJECT

To improvise a useful and inexpensive training aid, suspend a ball which can swing freely and can be raised and lowered to face height and knee height.

This is a smaller target than you would ordinarily hit in a defense situation. If you develop moderate facility in hitting the swinging ball you should have functional skill for striking a self-defense target.

65,66. Keep your eye on the ball. Practice hitting it with a series of consecutive hand blows. Do not strike with force; use a fast, light touch. If you hit the ball too hard it will swing wildly.

65

66

Practice various hand blows. Practice hitting with your right hand and your left hand. Practice to increase the number of times you can hit the target with a series of consecutive hand blows. In the beginning you may be able to hit the target few times without missing. When you can hit the ball with four or more consecutive blows without missing you will have developed adequate and functional skill.

Follow the ball with your eye instead of trying to chase it with your hand.

67

67. With the ball suspended at knee height, practice kicking at the target with various foot blows. Kick with your right foot and with your left foot. Practice to hit the target with light, accurate kicks. If you hit too hard the ball will swing too far.

Follow the ball with your eyes and your feet will learn to make contact with the target.

Another way to practice hitting a moving target is with a partner throwing a small beach ball.

In practice of responses to back attack it is important to look at the target area. Turn your back to the suspended ball and practice turn-as-you-hit hand blows. Practice turn-and-kick foot blows.

68

69

FULL-CONTACT STRIKING BAG

68,69. Full-contact blows can be practiced with a partner holding a striking bag. The training aid shown in the photo was improvised by filling a laundry bag with crushed newspaper.

Hit the bag with hand blows from different angles. Turn your back to the target and practice turn-and-hit hand and foot blows.

70

71

HITTING STICK

70,71. You can improvise a training aid by padding the end of a broom handle or long dowel with foam or with toweling. Fasten the padding with tape. For safety, do not use pins or metal clamps. The padded stick can be used to practice fully-released hand and foot blows.

72

HOOP STICK

72. Another improvised training aid can be made by fastening a loop of wire about six inches in diameter to the end of a dowel or broomstick. Do not leave sharp ends of wire exposed.

As your partner moves the hoop around -- slowly, at first -- practice aiming hand blows into the center of the moving target. As your responses become faster and more accurate the training hoop can be moved faster.

MEMORIZE TARGET AREAS

To prepare for those instances in which you might not be able to see the target clearly, you should practice to fix target areas in your mind as space relationships.

Assaults are more likely to occur in dark places than in lighted places. In dark or shadowy areas it is not possible to get sharp visual images.

Following are some practice procedures for memorizing body target areas.

73,74. Look at the target point and then turn away from it. Try to hit the target without looking at it. Space perception differs considerably from individual to individual; at first you may find that your perception of the location of the target is greatly distorted when you are not looking at it. Moderate practice should improve your ability to hit the target.

73

74

75

75. Mark a pole or stick with high and low target areas at approximately knee and neck height. Practice simultaneous hand and foot blows aimed at the exact targets marked on the pole.

76,77. Practice responding to cues other than visual ones. Blindfolded practice does not correspond to any particular assault; it is a training procedure to react to sound cues.

The "assault" cue is given by snapping fingers. When you hear the sound, simulate a blow aimed at the source of the sound.

76

77

FIGHTING STANCES: WHY & WHEN

In most instances fighting stances are not practical or possible for self-defense.

78. The standard boxing stance, of which there are many variations, provides a guard for the upper body but the lower body is unguarded.

This stance is quite appropriate for the sport of boxing. The sport is played by rules which prohibit and penalize hitting below the belt. It is therefore unnecessary to guard against low blows.

The terms "low blow" and "hitting below the belt" derive from the sport of boxing and they imply unfair and unsporting tactics. For self-defense, which is not a sport and in which there are no rules, low blows and hitting below the belt -- kicking into the knee or shin, for example – are efficient, practical and appropriate tactics for a small person defending against a larger assailant.

78

WRESTLING STANCE

79. When wrestling is played as a sport, the rules prohibit the use of hand or foot blows. Techniques are limited to grappling and takedowns for the purpose of applying a point-gaining hold. Because of these rules there is no need to put up a defense against blows to the body.

The open stance of the wrestler is appropriate to the activity.

But because of its open, unguarded aspect, this stance is not suitable for self-defense.

The parody of wrestling frequently seen on television is not wrestling as it is played in collegiate, national or world competition; it is a show put on to entertain the viewers.

79

JUDO CONTEST STANCE

80. Although in the past judo has been taught as a self-defense method, today it has taken its proper place as a sport; it is an event in the Olympic Games. Like wrestling, judo is played by rules which prohibit and penalize hand or foot blows or any tactic intended to hurt the opponent player.

Judo players do not use a fighting stance because there is no need to guard against the possibility of being struck.

Contestants in a judo match are in close contact, gripping cloth of the uniform as shown in the photo.

80

KARATE STANCES

There are many different stances taught in the various styles of karate. In traditional karate, stances are an important part of training and practice. For contest and tournament (the objective of most karate training) the stances are appropriate. It is my view that there are inherent drawbacks to karate stances for self-defense.

Self-defense is not a game. The purpose of using self-defense is not to win a point but to avoid becoming the victim of an assailant. If it is possible to accomplish that objective without fighting, so much the better.

There are many instances of threatened assault which can be handled and managed without any physical action -- verbal control and assertive behavior may be possible.

Taking a fighting stance eliminates the possibility of coping with hostility through negotiation or persuasion. It is easy enough to move from no physical action into physical action, if necessary, but it is very difficult to retreat from physical action once it has started.

Taking a fighting stance is a signal that you are ready for physical confrontation, that you are challenging the hostile individual and the action of taking the stance is more likely to provoke than it is to prevent.

In surprise situations, such as assault from behind, it is impossible to take a fighting stance. There may not be time to assume a fighting stance against a swiftly moving assault.

In those situations where physical confrontation is a possibility but not a certainty, I favor a guarded posture rather than a fighting stance. A guarded posture is any natural-looking position with your hands in front of you (ready to hit, if necessary) but not fisted, and with a strong stable foot position which allows you to shift body weight for kicking or for running!

81

81. This is the cat stance which is favored in some styles of karate. It is inherently a sport-fighting attack stance.

82. The horse stance, much favored by many styles of karate, is a strong and stable position. It is a good sport-fighting defensive stance.

83. This is a modified karate stance which offers high and low guards and permits quick shifting of body weight and ease of foot movement.

If physical confrontation is impossible to avoid, and there is time, and it seems appropriate to do so, a modified karate stance such as this one would be more practical than either the cat or horse stance. Or, you could take a boxing stance which has the advantage of concealing the style of your defense actions.

82

83

POINT TARGETS IN COMBAT SPORTS

The principal differences between sport matches and self-defense are: In contest or tournament the players are competing for points. They are usually of approximately equal skill and size. They have freely chosen to be opponents in a game which has rules to be observed by all participants.

Although the players in a sport fighting match might be hurt or injured, that is not the main objective of most combat sports. Even in boxing, a contest can be won by demonstrating superior technical skill, style and spirit -- without hurting the opponent.

In combat sports you can tell the winner from the loser by looking at the scoreboard.

Point targets in combat sports need not be those which are practical for self-defense. They may perhaps be symbolic of body targets aimed at in hand-to-hand warfare, but now modified for modern sport.

In fencing as it is presently played the point-gaining targets are touched, not cut. Because of the rules, the protective clothing and the objectives of the activity nobody gets killed in a fencing match.

Kendo is an excellent example of a classic Japanese combat skill which has evolved into a modern-day sport. Like fencing, kendo is based on ancient combat sword fighting. Today, a special stick made of split bamboo (*shinai*) is used to represent the sword.

The players use protective clothing and gear. The rules of kendo competition effectively eliminate the possibility of injury.

Skillful kendo players in tournament are exciting to watch. But the participants are enjoying the pleasure of physical activity and the thrill of competition without inflicting violence upon each other and without taking high risks of serious accidental injury.

Kendo target areas are onto the head, into the throat, the side of the body or head, and onto the wrist. These areas represent lethal sword cuts at vulnerable body targets. But because a *shinai* is used to represent the sword and the protective gear covers the head and neck and the waist and wrists, the contestants do not hurt each other. Thus, an ancient war skill has been completely modified to meet the requirements of modern sport. Technical skill, body discipline and style are demonstrated in kendo matches without risk of harm to the participants.

STYLES OF KARATE

Karate is commonly used as a generic term for the many styles and substyles of Asian methods of hand and foot fighting. There are dozens of styles of Japanese karate. Among the Chinese styles are Shaolin temple boxing, pa kua, kung fu (gung fu). The Korean styles include tai kwan do and hapkido.

Although all of the karate styles and methods use hand and foot blows as the principal techniques, there is considerable diversity among them in the manner of training, in the selection of preferred techniques, in the emphasis on either hand blows or foot blows, and in their utilization of prearranged routines (dances, kata) as practice procedures.

Some styles of karate do not include tournament training. In the styles which do not prepare for contest matches, solo practice and performance of one-man and two-man routines constitute the training method.

In some karate styles there is competition which consists of solo performance of routines to demonstrate the students' technical ability and formal skill.

There are other styles of karate in which contest matches are used as the principal method of developing skill and in which the training program is geared solely toward preparation for engaging in tournament.

There is a wide range of rules and regulations among the diverse karate groups. As is true in other competitive sports, there are a number of associations, none of which recognizes the legitimacy of the others. The champion of one karate association is not regarded as the champion by the others. The objectives of the various groups are also widely divergent. There is one faction moving toward dangerous, spectator-oriented, sensational, exploitive matches. Other groups are working toward the acceptance of karate as a modern sport geared to the health, physical development and physical well-being of the participants.

KARATE CONTEST POINTS

The traditional, old-style karate point-winning target areas are the most dangerous, high-risk-of-injury body areas. These targets reflect the original objective of karate fighting for hand-to-hand warfare, as do the target areas used in fencing and in kendo matches. But in karate there are insufficient safeguards against accidental serious injury.

The contest point targets in karate include head, throat and midbody. Some styles of karate allow the kidney region and the groin to be used as targets.

Some karate contests award points for unopposed blows which come very close to the target but do not touch it. The no-contact rule is supposed to prevent injury. Some karate contests allow contact blows but require the contestants to wear protective gloves. But in both cases -- no-contact or contact -- the blows are delivered into the unprotected, highly vulnerable body targets. Accidental or deliberate contact means high risk of serious injury.

KARATE MODERNIZED

If karate is to become a modern sport in the way that kendo and judo have become modern sports, there will have to be a change in the rules of contest. Protective gear worn by the contestants has proven cumbersome; it interferes with free and flexible movement. Clearly, it is the body target areas which should and could be changed.

It requires as much skill to touch or hit low-risk-of-injury target areas -- such as the upper arm, upper back or shoulder -- as it does to make points by aiming at the vulnerable areas now permitted in karate contest. Under the present rules accidental contact is dangerous. Changing the rules would improve karate by reducing the unneccesary risk without affecting the pleasure and excitement of tournament play for the participants.

In no-contact.contest, points are awarded for blows delivered very close to the target area, if the blow is unopposed by a blocking action. This would be a clear point.

But accidental contact often occurs because there is the possibility that the opponent is moving into the blow . . .

or because the players may not have the high skill which is needed for perfect control of their blows.

When the target areas are high-risk-of injury places, such as the eyes, the absence of perfect control in delivering close, no-contact blows. . .

results in forceful contact blows into the most vulnerable parts of the body. Accidental contact is dangerous.

Accidental contact to a low-risk-of injury target would reduce the possibility of injury to a considerable extent. If forceful contact were made, it would not have the effect of inflicting serious, irreversible injury.

Instead of delivering a kick into the groin area. . .

the upper leg could be substituted as the target for point-winning techniques. There would be no reduction of the required skill, but considerably less possibility of inflicting extreme and needless pain.

Kicking into the kidney and spleen region puts the contestants in extreme peril of dangerous blows....

When karate matches are played to entertain spectators the only attraction is the promise of dangerous thrills. Karate players who have prize money at stake may be willing to play that game, but physical education teachers are not going to encourage karate played as a performance for a blood-thirsty crowd.

Highly skilled karate players do not *often* make the mistakes which result in serious injury. But most of the people practicing karate are not highly skilled. By adopting new rules to ensure the safety of all the players karate contest could be made entirely consistent with the objectives of physical education and recreation programs for sport, fitness and health.

Specific rules for any contest are made by the sponsoring group. There is nothing to prevent any school or club from adopting health-and-safety oriented karate contest rules immediately.

as does kicking into the head as a contest tactic.

If the upper arm were made the target point for tournament, the sport of karate would become much safer.

HEAD

A – FRONTAL BONE
B – FRONTAL SINUS
C – NASAL BONE
D – NASAL CARTILAGE
E – HYDROID BONE
F – EPIGLOTIS
G – THYROID CARTILAGE
H – WINDPIPE (TRACHEA)
I – SECOND VERTEBRA (ATLAS)
J – FIRST VERTEBRA (AXIS)
K – OCCIPITAL BONE

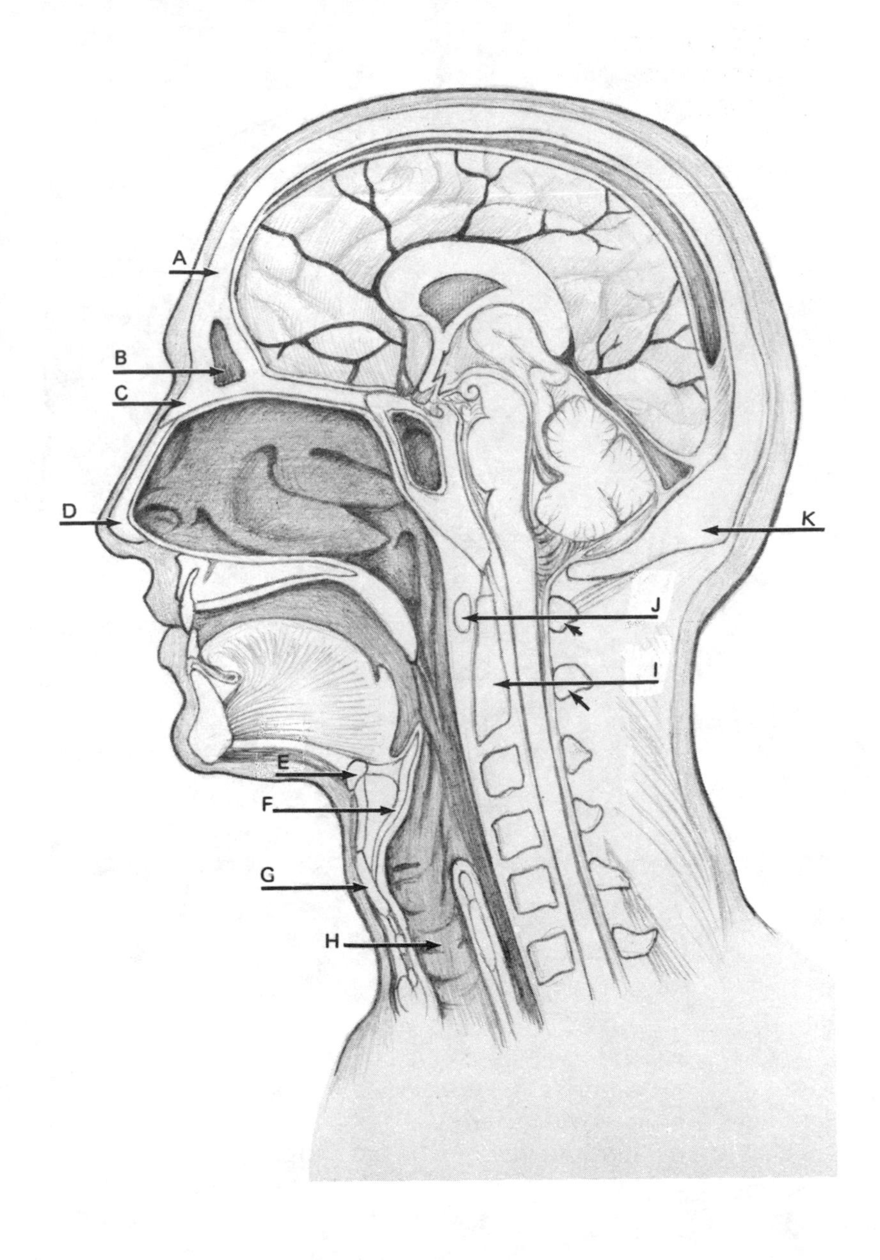
A
B
C
D
E
F
G
H
I
J
K

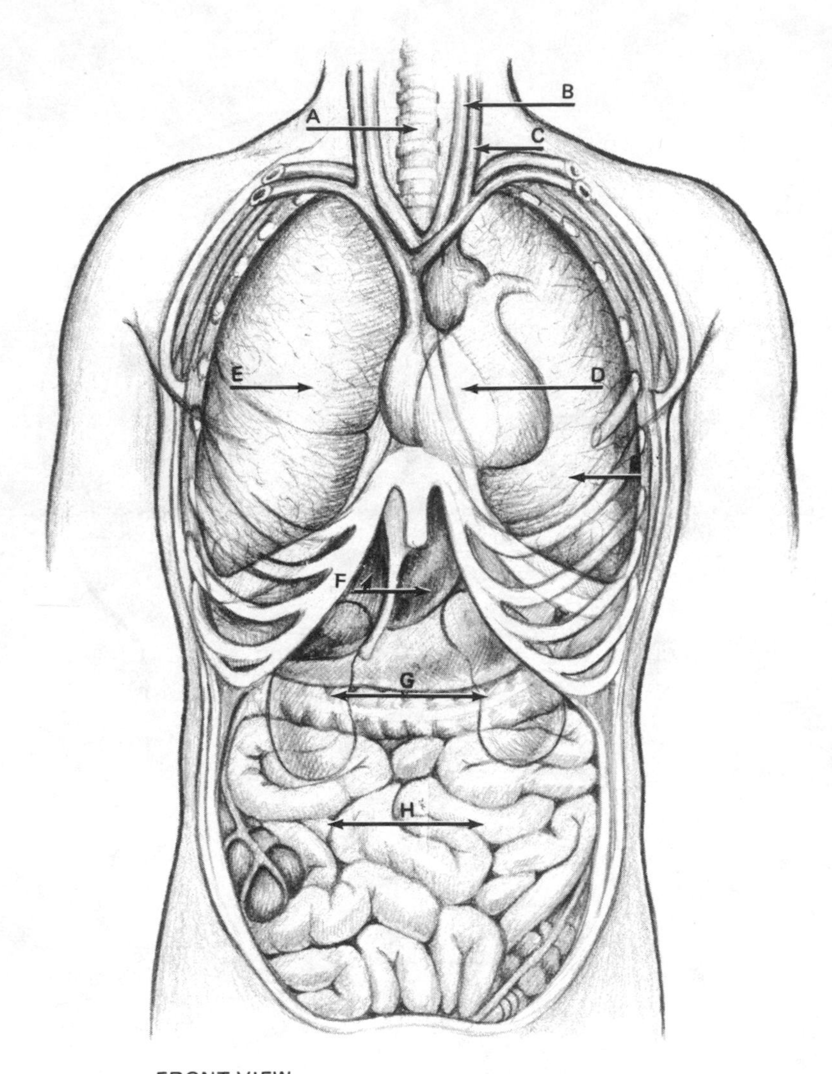

FRONT VIEW

A – WINDPIPE	E – LUNGS
B – CAROTID ARTERY	F – LIVER
C – JUGULAR VEIN	G – KIDNEYS
D – HEART	H – INTESTINES

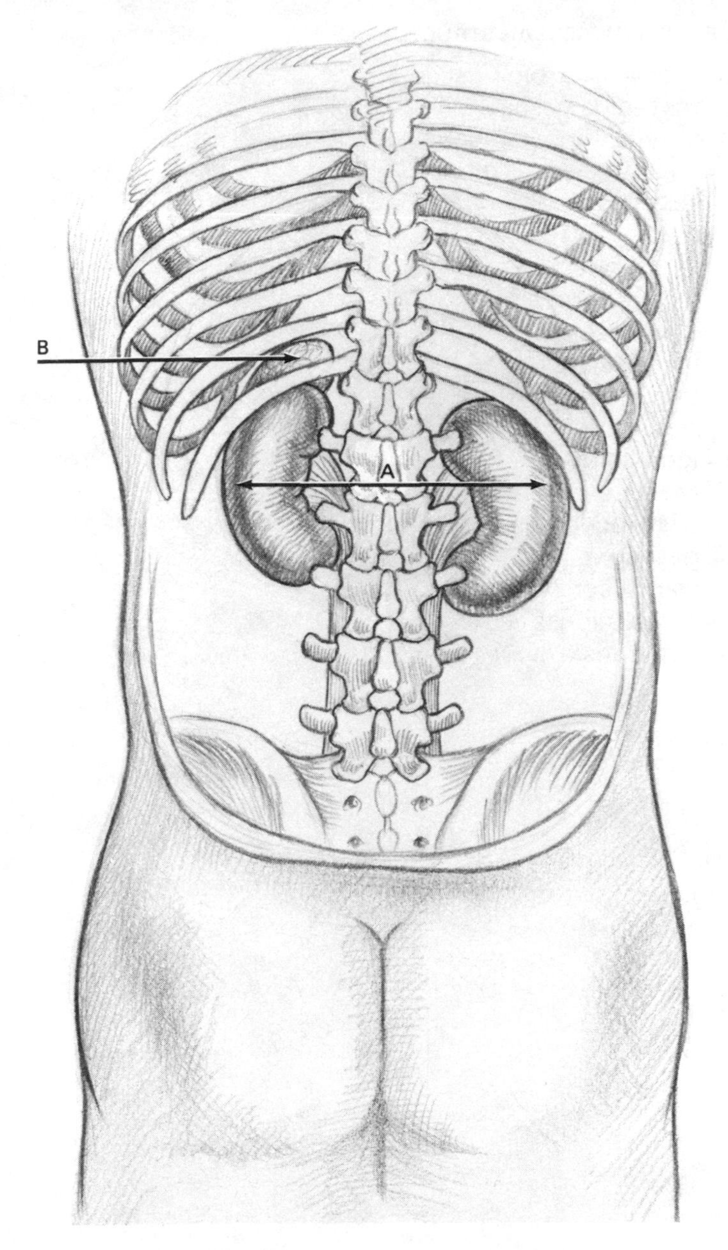

BACK VIEW A – KIDNEYS B – SPLEEN

SKELETAL/MUSCULAR STRUCTURE

A – STERNO-MASTOID MUSCLE
B – TRAPEZIUS MUSCLE
C – CLAVICLE (COLLARBONE)
D – STERNUM (BREASTBONE)
E – HUMERUS BONE
F – ELBOW JOINT
G – ULNA BONE
H – RADIUS BONE
I – PELVIC REGION
J – CARPAL BONES
K – METACARPAL BONES
L – FEMUR BONE
M – KNEE JOINT
N – PATELLA
O – GASTROCNEMIUS MUSCLE
P – TIBIA BONE
Q – FIBULA BONE
R – TARSAL BONES
S – METATARSAL BONES

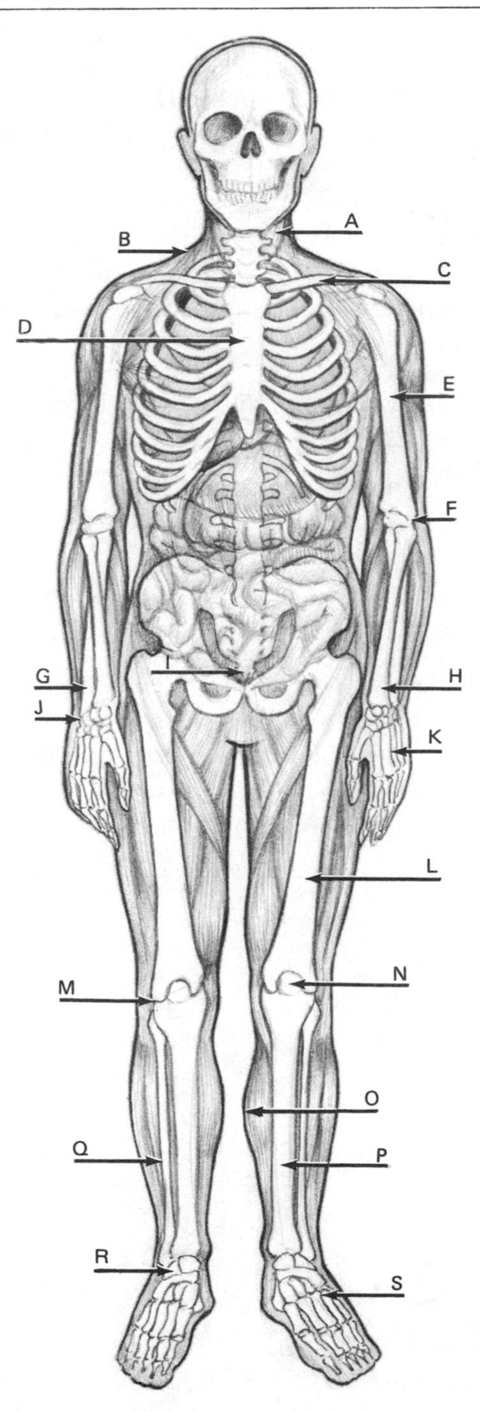
A
B
C
D
E
F
G
H
I
J
K
L
M
N
O
P
Q
R
S

TENDONS, LIGAMENTS & JOINTS

Another category of hand-to-hand fighting is that which operates on the principle of hyperextension -- bending , twisting (and sometimes striking at) the joints to force them beyond the normal range of movement. The effects of hyperextension range from moderate to extreme pain and include the possibilities of dislocation, stretching or tearing of the tendons or ligaments, and separation of the connective tissue.

As with any blow or tactic the results will vary with the circumstances -- the force of the action, the relative sizes of the individuals and the specific joint being hyperextended.

Aikido techniques are mainly hyperextensions of the wrist, elbow and shoulder joints. When aikido partners practice together, the "defending" partner will go with the action or roll with it in order to avoid pain or injury.

However, if the aikido technique shown in photo A were applied vigorously by a highly skilled individual against a person who did not go with the action, but instead *resisted* it, the combination of forceful pressure against the elbow joint and a snappy twist of the wrist could dislocate the elbow or sprain the wrist, or both.

A

The ability to apply this kind of technique with the degree of precision and the speed to make it effective can only be acquired through years of training and practice and can be maintained only with ongoing practice.

B

Many of the classic, old-style, traditional Asian self-defense methods included (indeed, still include!) tactics such as shown in photo B. In order to be able to apply this wrist-twist/ arm blow combination against a larger assailant, the smaller person would have to have an exceptionally high level of skill.

But not all of the hyperextension techniques are as difficult to learn and use as the ones shown in photos A & B. There are some simple applications of hyper-extension. The kick into the knee, discussed earlier in this text is one example.

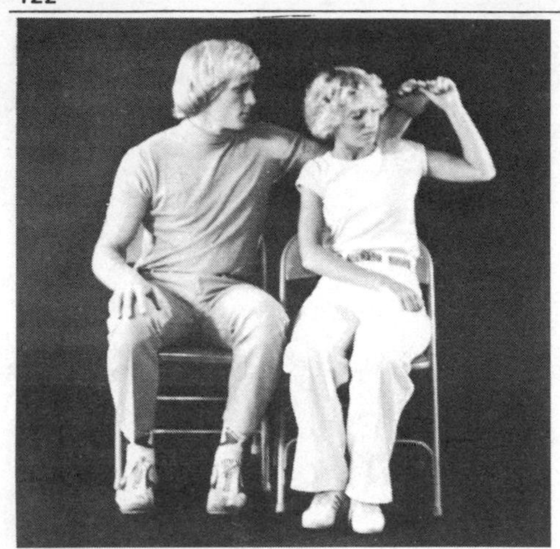

C

Another example is the easy-to-use, effective finger-bending action shown in photo C. With relatively little effort a finger can be hyperextended to cause pain and effect release.

D

For the lay citizen, control and restraint techniques like that shown in photo D have little relevance. Given proper and adequate training, professionals in law enforcement and related work can use them effectively.

INDEX

accuracy of descriptions 22
accuracy practice 88
aikido 120
anatomy, drawings 35, 115, 116, 117, 119
  importance of understanding 13
aortic arch 51, 52
archery 14
atemi-waza 14, 15
"best" targets 86
bladder 66
blindfolded practice 96
boxing 14, 15, 98
carotid artery hold 46
combat sports 104
comparing effects of blows 24
comparison of fighting systems chart 15
deadly blows 18
fencing 14
fight scenes in movies & television 32, 50
fighting systems compared 15
glasses 83
hand conditioning 21
hapkido 105
head 34, 50
hitting stick 92
hoop stick 93
judo 14, 15, 100
jugular vein 46, 116
jujitsu 14, 15
karate 14, 15, 20, 21, 101, 105
kata 105
kendo 14, 104
kung fu 15, 20, 40
ligaments 120
locating targets 82
martial arts, definition 14
media reporting 20
memory practice 94
movie & television fight scenes 32, 50
nerve centers, defined 12
nose bones into brain 18

pain 16
role in self-defense 17
pa kua 105
pressure points, defined 11
savate 14
self-defense, defined 11
self-defense nerve centers & pressure points
abdomen 66
Achilles' tendon 81
ankle 77, 84
arm, back of 62
body, side of 56
calf 80
chin 41
coccyx 78
collarbone 49
ear 42
elbow 58
eyes 40
forearm 60, 64, 84
groin 66
hand 65
instep 76
jaw 44
kidneys 53
knee 69
back of 72, 85
neck, base of 48, 50
side of 46, 84
nose 36, 38
shin 74
shoulder blades, between 52
skull, base of 50
solar plexus 54
temple 35
thigh 35
back of 78
throat
Adam's apple 43
hollow 44
windpipe 43
wrist 62

seven-year death 19
Shaolin temple boxing 105
spine, plucking out 19
spleen 117
stances
  boxing 98
  cat 102
  horse 102
  karate 101
  wrestling 99
striking bag 91
swinging ball 88
tai boxing 14
tai kwon do 105
targets, combat sports points 104, 113
techniques, classification of 14, 15
tendons 69, 81, 120
thyroid cartilage 43
trachea 43, 44
touch-of-death 19
vertebrae 50
weapons 26
windpipe hold, danger of 43
wrestling 14, 15, 99

BRUCE TEGNER was born in Chicago, Illinois in 1929. Both his parents were professional teachers of judo and jujitsu; they began his formal instruction in the martial arts when Bruce was two years old!

In a field where most individuals concentrate on a narrow specialty, Bruce Tegner's experience was unusual. His education covered many aspects of weaponless fighting of many styles, as well as sword and stick techniques.

At the age of twenty-one, after becoming the California state judo champion, he gave up competition to devote himself to research course development, teaching and teacher training.

In the U.S. armed forces Mr. Tegner trained instructors to teach unarmed combat; he taught military police tactics; he coached sport judo teams.

From 1952 through 1967 he operated his own school in Hollywood, California where he taught men, women, and children, exceptionally gifted students, and blind and disabled persons. He trained actors and choreographed fight scenes for movies and television. He devised special teaching methods and courses, some of which have been adopted by physical education departments and law enforcement training centers throughout the world.

Editions of Bruce Tegner titles have been published in German, Spanish, Portuguese, Dutch, and French.

BRUCE TEGNER books are on sale at bookstores and magazine stands throughout the world. If your local dealer does not stock the titles you want, you may order directly from the publisher.

For a free descriptive brochure, write to:

THOR PUBLISHING CO.
BOX 1782
VENTURA, CA. 93002